"Few men are endowed with the ability to motivate and effect changes in other human beings. Congratulations on the impact you're having on the people you touch . . ."

Tom Hopkins, President
Tom Hopkins International

"Jim Rohn will turn your life around. His seminars had a major impact on my personal development as well as the development of my business . . . I feel so strongly about Jim Rohn that I have everyone on my staff attend one of his seminars."

Louise Pomeroy, President and Founder
Abigail Abbott Personnel Company

"Jim Rohn is the most compelling, inspirational, and results-oriented leader and speaker of our time."

Earl Nightingale

"Jim Rohn's ideas and imaginative concepts for living and achieving are to the point . . . Better than that, they work!"

(Hon.) John Seymour
State Senator, California

"Everyone involved in the commercial process today needs to take stock. Jim Rohn has that rare ability to inspire people to set meaningful objectives for themselves . . ."

J.A. Hazlett, Marketing Director
Mobil Oil of New Zealand, Ltd.

Seven Strategies
for
Wealth and Happiness

How to Order:

Quantity discounts are available from: Prima Publishing and Communications, Post Office Box 1260R, Rocklin, CA 95677-1260; Telephone: (916) 624-5718. On your letterhead, include information concerning the intended use of the books and the number of books you wish to purchase.

Bookstores and libraries only: Prima Books are distributed to the trade by Interbook, Inc., 14895 E. 14th Street, Suite 370, San Leandro, CA 94577; Telephone: (415) 352-9221 — and in Canada, by Raincoast Book Distribution, Ltd., 112 E. 3rd Ave. Vancouver, B.C. V5Y 1K2. For all sales in other countries, contact Prima directly.

SEVEN
STRATEGIES
FOR
WEALTH
AND
HAPPINESS

JIM ROHN

Prima Publishing & Communications
Post Office Box 1260R
Rocklin, CA 95677-1260
Telephone: (916) 624-5718

(c) 1986 by Jim Rohn

Library of Congress Cataloging-in-Publication Data

Rohn, James E.
Seven strategies for wealth and happiness.

1. Finance, personal.   I. Title.   II. Title:
7 strategies for wealth and happiness.
HG179. R625   1985   650.1   85-19443
ISBN O-914629-02-6

1 2 3 4 5 6 7 8 9 10

Cover Design: Hatley Mason
Cover Photo: Courtland Llauger
Printed in the United States of America

To Yvonne, my inspiration

Contents

Acknowledgments

I wish to extend my deep gratitude to the editorial staff at Prima for preparing my Manuscript and turning it into the book it is today.

The Day That Turned My Life Around

Shortly after I turned twenty-five I met a man by the name of Earl Shoaff. Little did I know how this encounter would change my life . . .

Up until then my life had been embarrassingly typical of the vast majority of people who lead gray lives of little achievement and even less happiness. I *did* have a wonderful start, growing up in the loving environment of a small farming community in southwestern Idaho, just a short walk from the shores of the Snake River. When I left home I was filled with the hope of carving for myself a good-sized chunk of the American dream.

However, things did not turn out *quite* as I'd expected. After graduating from high school I promptly went to college. But at the end of one year I decided I was smart enough, so I quit. This turned out to be a major mistake — one of many major mistakes I would make during those early days. But I was impatient to work and to earn, figuring I wouldn't have any trouble getting a job, which turned out to be accurate. Getting a *job* wasn't hard. (I was yet to understand the difference between merely making a living and making a life.)

Shortly afterward, I got married. And like the typical husband, I made my wife lots of promises about the wonderful future which I *knew* was just around the corner. After all, I

3

was ambitious, I was very *sincere* about my desire to succeed, and I *did* work hard. Success was assured!

Or so I thought . . .

When I turned twenty-five, I had been working for six years, so I decided to take stock of my progress. I had a nagging suspicion that things weren't going quite right. My weekly paycheck amounted to a grand total of fifty-seven dollars. I was far behind in my promises and even further behind with the growing pile of bills strewn across our rickety kitchen table.

By now I was a father saddled with ever-growing responsibilities for my expanding family. But most of all I realized that gradually I had settled into quietly accepting my meager lot.

In a moment of honesty I began to see that rather than making progress I was falling further behind financially with each passing day. Something clearly had to change . . . but what?

Maybe hard work alone doesn't do it, I thought to myself. This, for me, was a shocking realization, raised as I was to believe that reward comes to those who earn their living by the sweat of their brow.

But it was plain as day that although I was "sweatin' plenty," I was on my way to ending up at age sixty like so many people I saw around me: broke and in need of assistance.

This terrified me. I couldn't face that kind of future. Not in this, the richest country in the world!

Still, I had more questions than answers. What should I do? How could I change the direction of my life?

I thought about going back to school. Only one year of college doesn't look good on a job application. But with a family to look after, going back to school seemed impractical.

Then I thought about starting a business. Now *that* was an exciting option! But, of course, I didn't have the needed capital.

After all, money *was* one of my biggest problems; I always had far too much month left over at the end of the money. (Have you ever been in that position?)

One day, I lost ten dollars. It upset me so much that I felt physically ill for two weeks — over a ten-dollar bill!

One of my friends tried to cheer me up. "Look, Jim," he said, "maybe some poor soul who needed it found it."

But believe me, that did *not* cheer me up. As far as I was concerned I was the person who needed to *find* ten dollars, not lose it. (I must admit that at that time in my life benevolence had not yet seized me.)

So that's where I was at age twenty-five — behind on my dreams without a clue as to how to change my life for the better.

Then one day good fortune came my way. Why did it appear at this point in my life? Why do good things happen when they do? I really don't know. For me, this is part of the mystery of life . . .

Anyway, my good fortune came when I met a man — a very special person by the name of Earl Shoaff. I first saw him at a sales conference where he was conducting a seminar. I cannot tell you what he said that evening that captivated me so, but I can still remember thinking to myself that I would give *anything* to be like him.

At the end of the seminar it took all the courage I could muster to just walk up to him and introduce myself. But in spite of my fumbling, he must have seen my desire to succeed. He was kind and generous and eventually took a liking to me. A few months later he hired me to join his sales organization.

For the next five years I learned many of life's lessons from Mr. Shoaff. He treated me like a son, spending hours teaching me his personal philosophy, which I now call the *Seven Strategies for Wealth and Happiness*.

Then one day, at age forty-nine, and without any warning, Mr. Shoaff died.

After mourning the loss of my mentor, I took some time to assess the impact he'd had on my life. I realized that the best thing I'd received from him was not a job or even the opportunity to grow from a sales trainee to executive vice-president of his company. Rather, it was what I'd learned from the wisdom of his philosophy of life and his fundamentals for successful living: how to be wealthy, how to be happy.

During the next few years I incorporated his ideas into my life . . . and I prospered. In fact, I made a great deal of money. But the most gratifying experience was sharing those ideas with my business associates and employees. The response was enthusiastic and the results immediate and measurable.

Although I saw myself as primarily a businessman and not as an author or speaker, I felt drawn to the challenge of communicating to others, simply and directly, those ideas that make a difference in how a person's life turns out.

As you read this book, imagine that you are shopping. Take and use only those ideas that apply to you now. You certainly don't have to "buy into" everything any one person says. But *do* give yourself a chance. Read the following pages with an open mind. If something makes sense to you, try it. If it doesn't, discard it.

Remember, in whatever you do be a student, not merely a follower.

Chapter 1

Five Key Words

All the ideas in this book stem from a group of key words. To understand this book, therefore, and to receive maximum value from its contents, it is essential that we reach agreement on the meaning of each one.

★ FUNDAMENTALS ★

First, let's take a look at the word "fundamentals." I define fundamentals as those basic principles on which all accomplishment is built.

Fundamentals form the beginning, the basis and the reality from which everything else flows.

It's a contradiction of terms to talk about *new* fundamentals. That's like someone claiming to have manufactured new antiques. One would be suspicious, right? No, fundamental principles belong to the ages. They have been the same from biblical times and will continue to remain so until the end of time.

Let's use the word "fundamentals" and apply it to the concept of success. If you are looking for *fundamental* success, the kind of success that lasts, that is built on a solid foundation, then you should avoid exotic answers. And believe me, there are lots of exotic answers being offered these days, especially in southern California where I live.

So in spite of rumors to the contrary, success is a simple process. It doesn't fall out of the sky. It is neither magical nor mysterious.

SUCCESS IS NO MORE THAN THE NATURAL CON-SEQUENCE OF CONSISTENTLY APPLYING THE FUN-DAMENTALS OF SUCCESS TO LIFE.

The same is true of happiness and wealth. They, too, are no more than the natural consequence of consistently applying the fundamentals of happiness and wealth to life.

The key is to stick to the fundamentals.

A Half-Dozen Things

Mr. Shoaff, my mentor, said to me one day, "Jim, there are always a half-dozen things that make eighty percent of the difference."

A half-dozen things . . . what a key thought.

Whether we are working to improve our health, wealth, personal achievement, or professional enterprise, the difference between triumphant success or bitter failure lies in the degree of our commitment to seek out, study, and apply those *half-dozen things*.

For example, for a farmer to reap a plentiful harvest in the fall, the half-dozen basics he must concentrate on are fairly obvious: soil, seed, water, sunshine, nourishment, and care. Each component is of equal importance because only *together* do they bring to fruition a successful harvest.

Thus, a good question to ask before undertaking any new project or setting new objectives is this: WHAT ARE THE HALF-DOZEN THINGS THAT WILL MAKE THE MOST

DIFFERENCE TO THE OUTCOME? Whether the enterprise is in the fine arts or in music, mathematics or physics, sports or business, it's those half-dozen fundamentals that count.

The understanding and application of this simple principle is the first intelligent step toward accomplishing your dreams and objectives.

★ WEALTH ★

The second key word to define is wealth. Wealth is a controversial word because it brings to mind a wide variety of images and sometimes conflicting concepts. After all, each of us views wealth from a different perspective. To one person, wealth may mean having enough money to do whatever he or she wishes. To another, it may mean freedom from debt — freedom from the constant claim of obligation. To yet another, it may mean the opportunity to grow and to achieve.

But out of this diversity comes creativity, and creativity can help each of us find unique ways to work for a life of abundance.

To the majority who probably haven't spent too much time thinking about the subject, wealth is simply symbolized by one word: *millionaire*. Now there's an exciting word! It rings of success, freedom, power, influence, pleasure, possibility, and benevolence. Surely, being a millionaire is not a bad mental image to hold!

Likewise, the word wealth embodies more than economic concepts. One can talk of the wealth of experience, the wealth of friendship, the wealth of love, the wealth of family, and the wealth of culture.

However, for our purposes here, we shall focus on the kind of wealth that brings with it financial freedom — WEALTH THAT COMES FROM THE CONVERSION OF EFFORT AND ENTERPRISE INTO CURRENCY AND EQUITY.

For each of us, the specific amount required for us to feel wealthy will differ. Yet I'm sure that our basic dream is the same: to be free of financial pressures, to have freedom of choice, and to enjoy the opportunity to create and to share.

What does wealth mean to you? How much money will it take for you to feel financially free? These are not idle questions. As you'll soon see, the more clearly defined your concepts about material wealth are, the more useful the ideas in this book will be to you.

★ HAPPINESS ★

Happiness embraces the universal quest. It's a joy that usually accompanies positive activity.

Like wealth, however, it, too, has a variety of often contradictory meanings. It's both the joy of discovery and the joy of knowing. It often accompanies those who are fully aware of the colors, sounds, and harmony of life.

And it's the joy that comes to those who painstakingly design their lives and then live them with artistry.

Happiness is the skill of reacting to the offerings of life by perception and by enjoyment.

It's achieved by both giving and receiving, reaping and bestowing. It's being able to feast on harmony as well as food, on ideas as well as bread.

Happiness comes to those who deliberately expand their horizons and experiences.

It resides in the houses of those who have the ability to handle disappointment without losing their sense of well-being. It belongs to those who are in control of both their circumstances and their emotions.

Happiness is also the freedom from the negative children of fear such as worry, low self-esteem, envy, greed, resentment, prejudice, and hatred.

Those who experience happiness often have a grasp on and an awareness of the tremendously positive power of life and love.

But happiness is more than a general feeling. It is also a *method of thinking* that organizes feelings, activities, and lifestyle. In other words, it's a way of interpreting the world and its events.

Happiness is having values in balance. It's contentment with daily tasks, including those unpleasant chores from which few of us are free.

Happiness is a life well-lived and filled with people of substance. It's a wide variety of experiences and memories that become priceless forms of currency to spend and to invest.

Happiness is activity with purpose. It's love in practice. It's both a grasp of the obvious and an awe of the mysterious.

Yet most of us think of happiness as something either lost in the past or a peak to be arrived at in some distant future (I'll be happy as soon as . . .). Few understand that happiness can only be experienced in the *now*. And, yes, like all good things, happiness is often elusive. But I promise you that it is *not* impossible to capture.

So how *does* one latch onto the bluebird of happiness? Curiously, by understanding and applying a concept which is rarely associated with happiness . . . discipline.

★ DISCIPLINE ★

If there is one critical ingredient for your successful quest for both wealth and happiness, it is discipline. And yet when it comes to this concept, most people reject it as they conjure images of everything from a tough drill sergeant to a strict schoolteacher waving a ruler.

Yet I assure you that the acquisition of discipline holds the key to your dreams and aspirations. Surprised? Then perhaps we should take a moment to define what is meant by discipline.

Discipline is the bridge between thought and accomplishment . . . the glue that binds inspiration to achievement . . . the magic that turns financial necessity into the creation of an inspired work of art.

Discipline comes to those with the awareness that for a kite to fly it must rise against the wind; that all good things are achieved by those who are willing to swim upstream; that drifting aimlessly through life only leads to bitterness and disappointment.

Discipline is the foundation on which all success is built. Lack of discipline inevitably leads to failure.

Yet, curiously, many do not associate lack of discipline with lack of success. Most people envision failure as one earth-shattering event, such as a company going bankrupt or a house being repossessed.

This, however, is not how failure happens. Failure is rarely the result of some isolated event. Rather, it is a consequence of a long list of accumulated little failures which happen as a result of too little discipline.

Failure occurs each time we fail to think . . . *today,* act . . . *today*, care, strive, climb, learn, or just keep going . . . *today.*

If your goal requires that today you write ten letters and you write only three, you are behind by seven letters . . . *today.*

If you commit yourself to making five phone calls and you make only one, you are behind by four phone calls . . . *today.*

If your financial plan requires that you save ten dollars and you save none, you are behind ten dollars . . . *today.*

The danger comes when we look at a day squandered and

conclude that no harm has been done. After all, it was *just* one day. But add up these days to make a year and then add up these years to make a lifetime and perhaps you can now see how repeating today's small failures can easily turn your life into a major disaster.

Success follows exactly the same pattern . . . in reverse. If you plan to make ten calls and you go beyond your quota to fifteen, you're ahead by five phone calls . . . *today*. Do the same with your correspondence and your savings plan and soon you'll see the *accumulated* fruits of your diligence over a year and, eventually, over a lifetime.

Discipline is the master key. It unlocks the door to wealth and happiness, culture and sophistication, high self-esteem and high accomplishment, and the accompanying feelings of pride, satisfaction, and success.

What does it take to acquire discipline?

First, it requires that you develop an awareness of the importance of discipline in your life. Start by asking yourself: "What do I want to accomplish in my life? What changes do I need to make in order to attain my goals?"

Second, ask yourself *honestly*: "Am I willing to do what it takes?" If you answer "yes," then you need to make a long-term commitment to maintain your discipline wisely, deliberately, *consistently*.

Finally, your commitment will be tested when circumstances emerge that could interfere with your commitment to your new discipline — when you will *have* to perform, come rain or come shine.

Certainly discipline will do much *for* you. But of even greater importance is what it will do *to* you. It will make you feel *terrific* about yourself.

Even the smallest discipline can have an incredible effect on your attitude. And the good feeling you get — that surging feeling of self-worth which comes from *starting* a new discipline — is almost as good as the feeling which comes from the *accomplishment* of the discipline.

A new discipline immediately changes the direction of your life, like a ship turning in mid-ocean and heading toward a new destination.

There are those who believe that discipline is unnatural — that just *being* is enough. They consider the need to accomplish to be a neurotic, man-made exercise. But the fact is that discipline cooperates with nature — where everything strives.

How tall will a tree grow? It fights the powerful force of gravity and keeps reaching toward sunlight to become as tall as it can be. True, this striving by a tree is not a conscious act — trees don't have brains. But *you and I* have been given the ability to consciously *choose* to strive and to become all that we can be.

Discipline attracts opportunity. Exciting opportunities invariably come to those who have developed skills and who have the ambition to act. And those who through discipline and commitment set their sights high will grab on to opportunities that forever remain unseen by more timid souls.

Discipline is that unique process of intelligent thought and activity that puts a lid on temper and a faucet on courtesy . . . that develops positive action and controls negative thoughts . . . that encourages success and refuses to accept failure . . . that promotes health and curbs sickness.

Anyone can begin the process of being disciplined. You can do it by degrees, one step at a time.

The exciting news is . . .

YOU CAN START . . . TODAY!

Don't say, "If I could, I would." Say instead, "If I would, I could . . . If I will, I can!"

So start the new process and start small. And then learn to stick with your new commitment. Out of this seemingly unimportant beginning you'll learn how it *feels* to be disciplined. And from there, the sky's the limit.

Action vs. Self-Delusion

In recent years there have been a number of books which promote the idea that if one verbally affirms what one wants on a daily basis, success will magically emerge.

I'm completely opposed to this mode of thinking. In my experience, affirmations without the discipline to act upon those things which are affirmed cause men and women to delude themselves into thinking they're making progress when, in fact, their daily activity leads them nowhere.

Why do people say one thing and then act in direct contradiction to their affirmations?

The man who dreams of wealth and yet walks daily toward certain financial disaster and the woman who wishes for happiness and yet thinks thoughts and commits acts that lead her toward certain despair are both victims of the false hope which affirmations tend to manufacture. Why? Because words soothe and, like a narcotic, they lull us into a state of complacency. Remember this: TO MAKE PROGRESS YOU MUST ACTUALLY GET STARTED!

So, to have a prosperous life, start a prosperity plan. To become wealthy, develop a "wealthy" plan. Remember, you don't have to be wealthy to have a wealth plan; a person without any means can have a "becoming rich" plan.

There are so many other types of plans which you can create:

● If you are ill, start a health plan.
● Do you feel tired all the time? Then start an energy plan.

- Feel a bit under-educated? That's right! Start an education plan.
- You say you can't? Then start an "I *can*" plan.

ANYONE CAN!

Even a bad person can start reading good books. The key is to take a step . . . *today*. Whatever the project, start TODAY.

Start clearing out a drawer of your newly organized desk . . . *today*.

Start setting your first goal . . . *today*.

Start listening to motivational cassettes . . . *today*.

Start a sensible weight-reduction plan . . . *today*.

Start calling on one tough customer a day . . . *today*.

Start putting money in your new "investment for fortune" account . . . *today*.

Write a long-overdue letter . . . *today*.

What the heck! Get some momentum going on your new commitment for the good life. See how many activities you can pile on your new commitment to the better life. Go all out! Break away from the downward pull of gravity. Start your thrusters going. Prove to yourself that the waiting is over and the hoping is past — that faith and action have now taken charge.

It's a new day, a new beginning for your new life. With discipline you will be amazed at how much progress you'll be able to make. What have you got to lose except the guilt and fear of the past?

Now, I offer you the next challenge: Make this — the first day of your new beginning — a part of the week of new beginnings.

Go ahead, see how many things you can start *and* continue in this, your week of new beginnings.

Then, make this the month of new beginnings . . . and then the year of new beginnings. By the time you've completed your first year you'll never again be claimed by the past — past habits, past influences, past regrets, past failures. As the Bible says, you'll now be ready to "fly with the eagles."

★ SUCCESS ★

Success is the fifth key word. And like each of the concepts already discussed, it has multiple layers of meaning.

Success is also an elusive notion, a paradox. After all, it is both a journey and a destination, isn't it?

It's the steady, measured progress toward a goal and the achievement of a goal.

Success is both an accomplishment and a wisdom that comes to those who understand the potential power of life.

It's an awareness of value and the cultivation of worthwhile values through discipline.

It's both material and spiritual, practical and mystical.

Success is a process of turning away *from* something in order to turn *toward* something better — from lethargy to exercise, from candy to fruit, from spending to investing.

Success is responding to an invitation to change, to grow, to develop, and to become — an invitation to move up to a better place in order to gain a better vantage point.

But most of all, success is making your life what *you* want it to be. Considering all the possibilities, considering all the examples of others whose lives you admire, what do *you* want from *your* life? That is the big question!

Remember, success is not a set of standards from our culture but rather a collection of personal values clearly defined and ultimately achieved.

Making your life what you want it to be for *you* — that is success. But how does one go about doing that? That's precisely what this book is about.

STRATEGY ONE

Unleash
the
Power
of
Goals

Chapter 2

Goals:
What Motivates People

One morning, two weeks after I started working for him, Mr. Shoaff and I were having breakfast together. Just as I was about to finish my eggs, he said, "Jim, let's take a look at your list of goals so that we can review and discuss them. Maybe that's the best way I can help you right now."

"But I don't have a list with me," I replied.

"Well, is it out in your car or at home somewhere?"

"No, sir, I don't have a list *anywhere*."

Mr. Shoaff sighed. "Well, young man, looks like this is where we'd better start."

Then, looking directly into my eyes, he said, "If you don't have a list of your goals, I can guess your bank balance within a few hundred dollars." He guessed right. And that *really* got my attention.

I was astonished. "You mean that if I had a list of my goals my bank balance would change?" I asked.

"Drastically," he said.

That day I became a student of the art and science of goal-setting.

Of all the things I've learned since those early days, goal-setting has had the most profound effect on my life. Every aspect of my existence — my accomplishments, my income, my bank balance, my lifestyle, my donations, even my personality — changed for the better.

I am so convinced that mastering goal-setting can have a profound effect on your life that I'm going to devote a great deal of space to discussing this often misunderstood process. In fact, I urge you to do more than just read the following chapters. Study them. And if you have a notebook handy, so much the better.

★ THE POWER OF DREAMS ★

Each and every one of our lives is affected by several factors. One of those factors is our environment — where we live, what kind of parents we have, which schools we attend, who our friends are; each plays a role.

We are also shaped by the events in our lives. A war, for example, can wrench all certainty from our psyche.

Knowledge, or the lack of it, will also shape our lives. So can the results of our efforts — we can either be elated or deflated based on our ability to achieve those desired results.

But of all the factors that affect our lives, none has as much potential power for doing good as our ability to dream.

Dreams are a projection of the life we wish to lead. Therefore, when we allow them to "pull" us, our dreams unleash a creative force that can overpower all obstacles hindering the attainment of our objectives.

To unharness this power, however, dreams must be well-defined. A fuzzy future has little pull power. To *really* achieve your dreams, to *really* have your future plans pull you, your dreams must be vivid.

Now, there are two ways to face the future: You can face the future with anticipation or you can face it with apprehension. Guess how many people face the future with apprehension? Right, most do.

You've seen the type — always worrying, worrying, *worrying*. Why are these individuals so apprehensive? Because they haven't spent time *designing* their futures. In many cases, they live their lives by trying to win the approval of someone else. In the process, they end up "buying into" someone else's view of how life should be lived. No wonder they are worried — always looking around, seeking approval for everything they do.

On the other hand, those who face the future with anticipation have planned a future worth getting excited about. They can "see" the future in their mind's eye, and it looks terrific. The future captures their imagination, and it exerts an enormous pull on them.

★ THE POWER OF WELL-DEFINED GOALS ★

Dreams are wonderful, but they are not enough. It's not sufficient to have a brilliant painting of the desired result. To erect a magnificent structure one must also have a step-by-step blueprint of how to lay the foundation, support the structure, and so on. And for that we need goals.

Like a well-defined dream, well-defined goals work like magnets. They pull you in their direction. The better YOU DEFINE them, the better YOU DESCRIBE them, the harder YOU WORK on achieving them, the stronger THEY PULL. And believe me when I say that when the "potholes" of life threaten to stall you on the road to *your* success, you'll need a strong magnet to pull you forward.

To understand how crucial goals are, observe the vast majority who do not have any goals. Instead of designing their lives, these misguided people simply make a living. They fight every day of their lives in the war zone of economic survival, choosing existence over substance. No wonder Thoreau said, "Most people live lives of quiet desperation."

★ REASONS ★

Mr. Shoaff said to me, "Jim, I don't think your current bank balance is a true indicator of your level of intelligence." (Boy, was I happy to hear that!) He continued, "I think you have plenty of talent and ability and that you're much smarter than you realize." And that turned out to be true; I *was* smarter than I thought at the time.

"Then why isn't my bank balance bigger?" I asked.

"Because you don't have enough *reasons* to accomplish," answered my friend. And then he added, "If you had enough motivation you could do incredible things; you have enough intelligence but not enough reasons."

A key thought, indeed: HAVE ENOUGH REASONS.

Since then I've discovered this: Reasons come first, answers second. It seems that life has a mysterious quirk of camouflaging the answers in such a way that they become apparent only to those who are inspired enough to look for them — who have reasons to look for them.

Let's put it another way. When you know what you want and you want it badly enough, you'll find a way to get it. The answers, methods, and solutions you need to solve the problems along the way will be revealed to you.

Hey, what if you *had* to be rich? What if the very life of someone you love *depended* on your being able to afford the very best medical care?

Let's further suppose that you just learned of a book or a

cassette tape that would show you how to make a fortune. Would you buy it? Of course you would!

Because you are already reading a book on success, it should come as no surprise to you that there are *many* good books and tapes on the subject of creating wealth. But if you don't *have* to be rich you probably won't read them or take the time to listen to them. There is an old saying, "Necessity is the mother of invention." How true! With that in mind, always work on your reasons first and the answers second.

★ FOUR GREAT MOTIVATORS ★

The big question you'll need to answer for yourself is: "What motivates me?"

Different things motivate different people. We all have our own "hot buttons." And if you do a bit of soul-searching, I'm sure you'll come up with a compelling list of your own.

What are some of the great motivators for excelling? Aside from the obvious desire for financial gain there are four other big motivators.

The first one is *RECOGNITION*. Great companies and savvy sales managers know that some people will do more for recognition than they will for material rewards.

That's why successful sales organizations, especially those involved in direct sales, take great pains to give recognition for any accomplishment, large or small. They know that in our overcrowded world most people feel that nobody cares, that they don't matter. And recognition is a kind of validation for their worthiness. In effect, those who recognize others are saying, "Hey, you are special, you make a difference."

I believe that if more companies took greater care to recognize their employees — not just the salespeople but also the executives, the secretaries, and the maintenance people — they would see an unbelievable surge in productivity.

The second reason some people excel is because they like the *FEELING* of winning. This is one of the best reasons.

If you must be addicted to something, make it an addiction to winning.

I have some friends, all millionaires, who still work ten to twelve hours a day making more millions. And it's not because they need the money. It's because they need the joy, the pleasure, and the satisfaction that come from their "wins." To them, money isn't the big drive; they already have plenty. You know what it is? It's the journey — the exhilarating *feeling* that comes from winning.

Once in a while, usually just after I give a seminar, someone will come up to me and say, "Mr. Rohn, if I had a million dollars I'd never work another day in my life." That's probably why the good Lord sees to it that people who say things like that never make a fortune. They would all just quit.

The third great motivator is *FAMILY*. Some people will do for their loved ones what they will not do for themselves.

I once met a man who told me, "Mr. Rohn, my family and I have a goal to travel around the world. To do everything we want to do will take a quarter of a million dollars a year." How incredible! Could a man's family affect him that much? And the answer is, "Of course!" How fortunate are those who are so profoundly affected by love!

BENEVOLENCE, the desire to share one's wealth, is the fourth great motivator. When the great steel magnate Andrew Carnegie died, his desk drawer was opened. Inside one of the drawers was a yellowed sheet of paper. On that slip of paper, dated from the time he was in his twenties, Carnegie had written the main goal for his life: "I am going to spend the first half of my life accumulating money. I am going to spend the last half of my life giving it all away."

You know what? Carnegie was so inspired by this that he accumulated 450 million dollars (which is equivalent to 4.5 billion dollars today!). And, indeed, during the last part of his life he had the joy of giving it all away.

★ NITTY-GRITTY REASONS ★

Wouldn't it be wonderful to be motivated to achievement by such a lofty goal as benevolence? I must confess, however, that in the early years of my struggle to succeed my motivation was a lot more down-to-earth. My reason for succeeding was more basic. In fact, it fell into the category of what I like to call "nitty-gritty reasons." A nitty-gritty reason is the kind that any one of us can have — at any time, on any day — and it can cause our lives to change. Let me tell you what happened to me . . .

Shortly before I met Mr. Shoaff I was lounging at home one day when I heard a knock at the door. It was a timid, hesitant knock. When I opened the door I looked down to see a pair of big brown eyes staring up at me. There stood a frail little girl of about ten. She told me, with all the courage and determination her little heart could muster, that she was selling Girl Scout cookies. It was a masterful presentation — several flavors, a special deal, and only two dollars per box. How could anyone refuse? Finally, with a big smile and ever-so-politely, she asked me to buy.

And I wanted to. Oh, how I wanted to!

Except for one thing. I didn't *have* two dollars! Boy, was I embarrassed! Here I was — a father, had been to college, was gainfully employed — and yet I didn't have *two dollars* to my name.

Naturally I couldn't tell this to the little girl with the big brown eyes. So I did the next best thing. I lied to her. I said, "Thanks, but I've already bought Girl Scout cookies this year. And I've still got plenty stacked in the house."

Now that simply wasn't true. But it was the only thing I could think of to get me off the hook. And it did. The little girl said, "That's okay, sir. Thank you very much." And with that she turned around and went on her way.

I stared after her for what seemed like a very long time. Finally, I closed the door behind me and, leaning my back to it, cried out, "I don't want to live like this *anymore*. I've *had it* with being broke, and I've *had it* with lying. I'll *never* be embarrassed again by not having any money in my pocket."

That day I promised myself to earn enough to always have several hundred dollars in my pocket at all times.

This is what I mean by a nitty-gritty reason. It may not win me any prize for greatness, but it was enough to have a permanent effect on the rest of my life.

My Girl-Scout-cookie story *does* have a happy ending. Several years later, as I was walking out of my bank where I had just made a hefty deposit and was crossing the street to get into my car, I saw two little girls who were selling candy for some girls' organization. One of them approached me, saying, "Mister, would you like to buy some candy?"

"I probably would," I said playfully. "What kind of candy do you have?"

"It's almond roca."

"*Almond roca*? That's my *favorite*! How much is it?"

"It's only two dollars." *Two dollars*! It couldn't be!

I was excited. "How many boxes of candy have you got?"

"I've got five."

Looking at her friend, I said, "And how many boxes do *you* have left?"

"I've got four."

"That's nine. Okay, I'll take them all."

At this, both girls' mouths fell open as they exclaimed in unison, "Really?"

"Sure," I said. "I've got some friends that I'll pass some around to."

Excitedly, they scurried to stack all the boxes together. I reached into my pocket and gave them eighteen dollars. As I was about to leave, the boxes tucked under my arm, one of the girls looked up and said, "Mister, you're really something!"

How about that! Can you imagine spending only eighteen dollars and having someone look you in the face and say, "You're really something!"

Now you know why I always carry a few hundred dollars on me. I'm not about to miss chances like that ever again.

Let me give you another example of a nitty-gritty reason for wanting to do well. I have a friend by the name of Robert Depew. Bobby used to be a schoolteacher in Lindsay, California, the olive capital. After several years as a teacher Bobby was looking forward to making a break and starting a new career. One day, without telling anyone, he quit teaching and jumped into sales. When his family found out about it he became the butt of lots of criticism. But the worst reaction came from his brother, who seemed to be getting great pleasure from harassing him.

"You're going to go right down the drain," mocked his brother. "You had a good teaching job. Now you're gonna lose everything you've got. You must be outta your mind."

Bobby's brother kept taunting him every chance he had. As Bobby relates, "The way my brother acted made me *so* angry that I decided to get rich."

Today, Bobby Depew is one of my millionaire friends.

This story, as well as my own "cookie" story, demonstrate that even anger and embarrassment, when properly channeled, can act as powerful nitty-gritty motivators to achieve.

Do you have something to prove? Do you have some old embarrassment you want to wipe off the slate? You know, that old saying "Massive success is the sweetest revenge" is true.

As you can see, there are almost as many reasons for people to do well as there are people. The key is to HAVE ENOUGH REASONS. How does one find the "hot button" (or buttons) that can transform a life of modest accomplishment into a life of wealth and happiness? That's the subject of the next chapter.

Chapter 3

Goals:
How to Set Them

In chapter one we discussed the importance of discipline. And now I'm going to ask you to start exercising this positive trait.

If you haven't yet done so, get out a notebook or a diary. I want you to transform yourself from spectator (reader) into participant (writer).

The kind of homework you're about to do here is a little unusual in that it lasts a lifetime. The subject is goals, and as you'll soon learn, goals are a lifelong preoccupation — ever-evolving, ever-changing.

Why should you put yourself through this? Because by doing the work involved you're taking the first steps toward developing the kind of life you've always dreamed about but never believed would happen for you. So let's get on with it. The sooner you exert the discipline, the sooner you'll enjoy the results. And once the results come in, I promise you won't mind one bit that it took some extra work and discipline.

★ LONG-RANGE GOALS ★

In your notebook or on a sheet of paper, write the heading,

"Long-Range Goals." Your task is to answer the question, "What do I want within the next one to ten years?"

The key to doing this exercise effectively is to take as *little* time as possible writing down as many items as possible. Take between twelve to fifteen minutes for the whole exercise, and try to write down about fifty different items.

To help you get started, consider the following half-dozen questions as guidelines:

1. What do I want to do?

2. What do I want to be?

3. What do I want to see?

4. What do I want to have?

5. Where do I want to go?

6. What would I like to share?

With these half-dozen queries in mind, answer the primary question: "What do I want within the next one to ten years?" Allow your mind to free-flow. Don't try to be detailed now; this will come later. For instance, if you want a gray Mercedes 380SL with a blue interior, just write "380" and move on to the next item.

After you have completed your list, review what you've written.

Next put the number of years you believe it will take for you to achieve or to acquire each item on your list. Next to the items you think you'll reach in a year or so, write the number "1." Next to the goals you believe will take approximately three years to accomplish, write the number "3." Next to those you think will take five years, write "5." And finally, next to those items you estimate will take ten years to attain, write "10."

Now, check to see if your goals are in balance. For example, if you find that you have lots of ten-year goals but very few one-year goals, this could mean you're putting off having to act now by postponing the target date.

On the other hand, if you have very few long-term goals, perhaps you haven't yet decided what kind of life you want to build over the long run.

The key here is to develop a balance between shorter-term and longer-term goals. (A little later we'll discuss true short-term goals. These are goals that take less than a year to accomplish.)

Are you a bit bewildered by the idea of having too many goals? Are you the kind of person who is more comfortable focusing on one goal at a time?

Actually, there is a good reason for developing multiple layers of goals. Without many and varied types of goals, you could fall prey to the same thing that happened to some of our early Apollo astronauts. Some of them, upon returning from the moon, experienced deep emotional problems. The reason? Once you've been to the moon, where else do you go?

After years of training, visualizing, and anticipating the lunar flight, that moment, glorious as it was, was gone. All of a sudden there seemed to be an end, a finish to their life's work, and depression set in.

As a result of this experience, later astronauts were trained to have other major projects "on the fire" after their space work was done.

Happiness is elusive. It seems that the best way to enjoy life is to wrap up one goal and simultaneously begin work on the next one. It's dangerous to linger too long at the table of success. The only way to enjoy another meal is to get good and hungry.

All right, now that you've reviewed and balanced your list, choose the four goals from each of the four time categories (one-year, three-year, five-year, ten-year) that you consider the most important to you. You now have sixteen goals. For each, write a short paragraph which includes the following:

1. A detailed description of what you want. For example, if it's a material object, describe how high, how long, how much, what model, what color, and so on. On the other hand, if it's a position or a business you want to start, give a detailed job description including salary, title, budget under your control, number of employees, and so on.

2. The reason *why* you want to achieve or acquire the item described. Here you'll find out if you *really* want it or if it's just a passing fancy. If you can't come up with a clear and convincing reason why you want it, you should categorize this item as a whim, not as a true goal, and replace it with something else.

You see, *what* you want is a powerful motivator *only* if there is a good reason behind it. You may find that some goals you once considered important no longer have appeal simply because you are unable to find a good enough reason for wanting them. That's good. Doing this assignment is causing you to reflect, refine, and revise. And that's the whole point behind this: to help you plan your future.

Once you have settled on your sixteen goals, copy them onto a separate sheet of paper or into a permanent journal and carry them with you at all times. Review them once a week to see if they're still important and if you are taking active steps toward their realization. As you can see, goal-setting is not a one-time task with the results set in concrete. Instead, it's a continuous, lifelong process.

★ SHORT-TERM GOALS ★

I define short-term goals as those which take anywhere from a day to a year to achieve. And these goals, although by necessity they are more modest than long-term goals, are of equal importance. A ship captain may set his long-range course toward his final destination, yet along the way there are many short-range points of arrival which must be reached for the voyage to be successful.

Now, just as in the case of a sea voyage, the short-term goals must be related to your long-term achievements. But they have the distinct advantage of being reachable in the foreseeable future. I call these kinds of goals "confidence builders" because their accomplishment gives you confidence to go on. So when you work hard, burn the midnight oil, and complete a specific, short-term task, you can enjoy your "win" and be re-inspired to continue your journey.

That's why I urge you to write down in your notebook or journal your short-range projects as well. How you organize this is up to you. You may, for example, arrange them by day, by week, or by month. Or you may position them as sub-categories of your long-term goals.

Part of the fun of having a list is the ability to check things off. And when you check something off as completed, take time to celebrate your achievement. This celebration could be a moment of satisfied reflection when you finish a small task or a major reward when the accomplishment calls for it. Regardless, *do* take time to enjoy your victories. It will only inspire you to do more.

But just as I urge you to partake of the heady wine of success, I have another, less popular recommendation: MAKE LOSING PAINFUL.

You see, we grow from two kinds of experiences: the joy of winning and the pain of losing. So if you set yourself on course to complete a project and you fooled around instead, find a way to pay for your laziness. Take responsibility for both positive and negative behavior.

In addition, surround yourself with people who won't put up with your usual baloney. Don't join an easy crowd. Go where the expectations are high, where the pressure to perform is high. That, too, is part of your overall strategy for wealth and happiness.

★ SLIDING ★

I want you to succeed! That's why I'm a little concerned. You see, I know that most of those who read these pages won't persist in setting and refining their goals. Why? Because it's time-consuming, thought-demanding work. And yet, it's ironic that the many men and women who work hard day in and day out at jobs they don't necessarily like, when asked to take time to design their own futures, often reply, "I don't have the time." They let *that*, their future, slide.

I know that *most* people don't make definite plans, but don't *you* be a part of that *most*. Don't *you* go around with your fingers crossed and a worried look on your face, *hoping* things will get better.

Whether you accept it or not, you are, right now, one of the players in the game of life. And believe me, if you don't have goals to shoot at, you aren't playing a very exciting game. No one will pay good money to watch you play a game where nobody's keeping score.

The "guy" says, "You work where I work, by the time you

get home it's late. You've got to have a bite to eat, watch a little TV to relax, and get to bed. You can't sit up half the night and plan, *plan*, PLAN." And this is the guy who's behind on his car payments. He's a good worker, a hard worker, a *sincere* worker.

But, friends, I've discovered that you can be *sincere* and work hard all your life and wind up broke and embarrassed. You've got to be better than a good worker. You've got to be better than sincere. You've got to be a good planner, a good goal-setter.

Writing your goals down shows that you're committed to growth, that you're serious. And to do better you've got to get serious. You don't have to be grim, but you *do* have to be serious. Hey, everybody *hopes* to do better. But hope, unaided by clear planning, can actually hurt you. As the Bible says, "Hope long delayed makes the heart sick." It's a sickness . . . I know.

I used to suffer from the illness known as passive hope. It's bad. The only thing worse than passive hope is *happy* passive hope. That's when a man is fifty and broke, and he's still smiling and hoping. Now that's *really* bad. So get serious. Put your goals on paper. My suggestion to you — from experience.

Chapter 4

Goals:
Making Them Work for You

The Bible says, "Without dreams and vision, we perish."
How true! But you know, the opposite is also true. With dreams
we can be transformed in unique and unprecedented ways. In
the previous chapters I showed you how to choose your goals
and to start reaching for them. Now you'll learn how to let
your dreams mold your very existence.

First, you need to understand that once you set goals that
really matter to you, you are no longer the same person. Real
goals will affect almost everything you do all day long. And
they will be with you wherever you go. Your handshake, your
manner of dressing, the tone of your voice, the way you feel
— all will change once you have goals. That's because when
your goals matter, everything you do becomes related to their
accomplishment.

But for goals to really *move* you, to take charge of your
life, they must be worthy. I once asked a man, "What are your
goals for the month?" He said, "If I could just scrape up enough
money to pay these lousy bills . . ." *That* was his goal!

Now I'm not saying that paying the bills can't be a goal —
it can. But it's such a *poor* goal. I certainly wouldn't put it on

the list of life's most inspiring motivations. You don't jump out of bed on Monday morning and say, "Oh, boy, another chance to go out there and scrape up enough money to pay these lousy bills."

To have your goals transform you, you must set them high. Set them enough out of reach to cause you to grow and to stretch; set them high enough to excite your imagination and motivate you to action. But just as you must set them high enough to *pull* you, don't set them so far beyond you that you lose heart before you begin.

★ THE TRUE PURPOSE OF GOALS ★

Let me share with you an intriguing thought. The real value in setting goals is *not* in their achievement. The acquisition of the things you want is strictly secondary. The major reason for setting goals is to *compel* you to become the person it takes to achieve them. Let me explain:

What do you think is the greatest value in becoming a millionaire? Is it the million dollars? I don't think so. No, the greatest value is in the skills, knowledge, discipline, and leadership qualities you'll develop in reaching that elevated status. It's the experience you'll acquire in planning and developing strategies. It's the inner strength you'll develop to have enough courage, commitment, and willpower to attract a million dollars.

Give a million dollars to someone who does not possess the *attitude* of a millionaire and that person will most likely lose it. But take away all the wealth from a *true* millionaire and in no time he or she will build a new fortune. Why? Because those who *earn* their millionaire status develop the skills, knowledge, and experience to duplicate the process again and again.

As you can see, when someone becomes a millionaire, the *least* important thing is what they have. The *most* important thing is what they have become.

Here's a question you should spend some time pondering: What kind of person will you have to become to get all you want? In fact, why not write down a few thoughts on this in your notebook or journal. Write down the kinds of skills you'll need to develop and the knowledge you'll need to gain. The answers will give you some new goals for personal development.

Remember this rule: INCOME RARELY EXCEEDS PERSONAL DEVELOPMENT. That's why all of us must subject ourselves to self-examination.

I often look at my life and ask, "Well, here's what I want, but am I willing to become the kind of person it will take?" If I'm too lazy, if I'm not willing to learn, read, study, and grow to become what I must become, then I cannot expect to attract what I want. Now, when faced with a choice, I must decide to either change myself or change my wants.

★ DON'T BECOME OVERWHELMED ★

When setting goals, especially for the first time, it's easy to become overwhelmed by the process. My advice to you is, relax.

If you don't feel you're equipped to get what you want, remember this: YOUR ABILITY WILL GROW TO MATCH YOUR DREAMS. This is the magic of goal-setting. The more you work on your goals, the more new opportunities will present themselves to you. And inside each new opportunity will be the seed of solution to a previous, seemingly unsolvable problem.

So don't be afraid to get started. The journey will take you far beyond your wildest imagination. I know. The person I was twenty-five years ago when I met Mr. Shoaff is, today, a stranger to me. I am no longer that person. I've changed. So can you.

Many people are afraid to get going because of past failure and pain. They carry heavy burdens on their souls, burdens that unless unloaded will weigh them down forever.

My friend, there is nothing you and I can do about the past. It's gone and buried. But you can do a great deal about your future. You don't have to be the person you were yesterday. You can make changes in your life — absolutely startling changes in a fairly short period of time. You can make changes you can't even conceive of right now, if you just give yourself half a chance.

Your abilities *will* grow. You'll draw on untapped potential and talents that you never knew existed. And as time goes on, you'll draw from new reserves deep within your creative mind. Before you know it, you'll be able to accomplish things that now seem impossible to achieve. You'll be able to handle things you never thought you could handle. Your mind will give birth to new and creative ideas.

Why are goals so powerful? How can they cause all this to happen? I don't know. I guess this question falls into that special category I call "the mysteries of life." All I can tell you is that it *does* work. Find out for yourself. Give yourself the chance to become all you can become and to accomplish all you can accomplish.

★ ASKING ★

There's a command in the Bible that teaches all you need to know to get what you want. This is what it says: "Ask."

That's it — *ask*. Of all the important skills to learn, make sure that you've got this one down.

What does "ask" mean? Ask means "ask for what you want." And the complete formula is staggering. It is: "Ask, and you shall receive." I think we'd better look into that . . .

First, asking starts the process of receiving. Asking is like pushing a button that unleashes incredible machinery, both intellectual and emotional.

As I said before, I don't know how or why it works, but I do know it works.

There are a lot of things that work equally well whether we understand the mechanism behind them or not. Just work them! Some people never get started because they're always studying the roots. And then there are others who choose to pick the fruit while they study the roots. It all depends on which end you want to start with. I recommend that you start asking.

Second, receiving, the other part of the formula, is not a problem. You don't have to work on receiving. It's automatic. So if receiving isn't difficult, what's the problem? It's failing to ask.

The "guy" says, "Yes, but you work where I work, by the time you struggle home it's late. You've got to get a bite to eat, watch a little TV to relax, and then get to bed. You can't sit up half the night and ask, *ask*, ASK." And this fellow is behind on his bills. He's a good worker, a hard worker, a *sincere* worker. But you've got to do better than work hard and be sincere all your life, or you'll wind up broke and embarrassed. You've got to be better than a good worker. You've got to be a good asker.

"I see it now," he says. "I got up every day this past year and hit it hard. But nowhere in my house is there a list of the things I ask of life."

How about you . . . how is *your* list?

Third, receiving is like the ocean — there's plenty. This is especially true in this country. It's like an ocean here! Success is not in short supply. It isn't rationed so that when your turn comes they already gave it all away. No, no!

If that's true, what's the problem? The problem is that most people go to this ocean of opportunity with a teaspoon. Have you got the picture? A *teaspoon*! In view of the size of the ocean, may I suggest that you trade in your teaspoon for something bigger? How about a pail? It may not be the best you can do, but at least kids won't make fun of you . . .

Two more thoughts about asking . . .

First, ask with intelligence. The Bible may not say, "Ask intelligently." But I have no doubt that this is what is meant. So don't mumble. You won't get anything by mumbling. Be clear . . . be specific. Asking intelligently includes answering how high, how long, how much, when, what size, what model, what color. Describe what you want. Define it. Remember, well-defined goals are like magnets. The better you chisel them, the stronger they pull.

Second, ask with faith. Faith is the childlike part. It means believe that you can get what you want. Believe as a child believes. Believe without the skepticism and cynicism of the adult in you.

You see, many of us have become *too* skeptical. We've lost that wonderfully innocent, childlike faith and trust. Don't let this stop you. Believe in and have faith in yourself and your goals. And get excited — just like a child. Childlike enthusiasm — there's nothing more contagious.

Children think they can do anything. They want to know about everything. How wonderful! They hate to go to bed at night and can't wait to jump out of bed in the morning. Children can ask a thousand questions. And just when you think you're ready to climb the wall, they'll ask a thousand more. They will drive you to the brink. But, of course, their curiosity is really a virtue. When you rekindle your own childlike sense of curious enthusiasm, you will be well on your way to becoming a masterful asker.

★ GOAL-SETTING AND TIME MANAGEMENT ★

Time management is a popular topic these days. All kinds of books, tapes, and seminars are offered to a public that is hungry for information on how to use time more productively.

How about you? Would you like to become a better time manager? Then you need to understand this: UNLESS YOU HAVE GOALS, IT IS IMPOSSIBLE TO MANAGE YOUR TIME EFFECTIVELY. Productivity is a result of well-defined objectives. The allocation of time is not critical if objectives are not firm and vividly planted in the mind. It's that simple. This is one of the many reasons why writing goals down on paper is so important.

★ PRIORITIES ★

One of the difficulties we face in our industrialized age is the fact that we've lost our sense of seasons. Unlike the farmer whose priorities change with the seasons, we have become impervious to the natural rhythm of life. As a result, we have our priorities out of balance. Let me illustrate what I mean:

For a farmer, springtime is his most active time. It's then that he must work around the clock, up before the sun and still toiling at the stroke of midnight. He must keep his equipment running at full capacity because he has but a small window of time for the planting of his crops. Then comes winter when there is less for him to do to keep him busy.

There is a lesson here. Learn to use the seasons of life. Decide when to pour it on and when to ease back, when to take advantage and when to let things ride. It's easy to keep going from nine to five year in and year out and lose a natural sense of priorities and cycles. Don't let one year blend into another in a seemingly endless parade of tasks and responsibilities. Keep your eye on your own seasons, lest you lose sight of value and substance.

Majors and Minors

An important part of setting priorities is learning to separate the minors of your life from the majors. Here is a good question to ask yourself whenever you have to make a decision. Is this a major or a minor? By asking this, always with your goals in mind, you'll reduce the risk of spending major time on minor projects.

In sales we are taught that there exists only one major time. That's the time we spend in the presence of a prospect. Any time spent on the way to the prospect, no matter how essential, is minor time. Too many salespeople spend more time "on the way to" than "with." And their incomes reflect this. That's why in sales we teach, "Don't go across town until you've gone across the street."

The majors and minors concept has another application. It also says, don't spend minor time on major things. It's easy to get values all mixed up. A parent spends three hours watching TV and only ten minutes playing with the children. A manager spends most of the day filling out forms and very little time encouraging his employees. These are people who have lost a sense of what's important and what's trivial.

This same concept also applies to money. Don't spend major money on minor things, and, conversely, don't spend minor money on major things. Some people spend a fortune on food for their bodies and very little on food for their minds. If you spend more on candy than on inspirational books and tapes, that would be foolish, right?

The best use of time and money comes from putting maximum *value* in it. It's called careful investment for maximum results.

★ CONCENTRATION ★

Any professional athlete can tell you about the horrible costs of lack of concentration. Just a momentary slip of concentration and "they put one by your feet." And there goes first place and the big money. Don't let it happen to you.

Put maximum attention to everything you do. When you write a letter, concentrate. Trying to solve a problem? Concentrate. Having a conversation? That's right, concentrate. You won't believe the effect this will have on your life.

Naturally, there is a time to let your mind wander. But do it during a period that you've set aside especially for doing just that. And when you wander, do nothing else. Go off for that walk on the beach or that drive in the mountains — away from the pressures of life. Let the breeze blow through your hair and let your mind soar. Daydream. That's good for you. But do it only at the time you designate as "daydreaming time." At all other times, concentrate.

★ A DOSAGE OF REALITY ★

There is a last point to consider . . . Even with the most

carefully thought-out plan of action, you won't get everything you want. I know. How can I possibly say this after spending so much time showing you how to get everything you want? Am I speaking from both sides of my mouth?

Why *won't* you get everything you want? Because, my friend, it's not that kind of world. Sometimes it will hail on your crop and rain on your parade. Sometimes the termites of life will gnaw at your foundations. It's not fair, you say? Perhaps not. But because you and I were not consulted in the initial planning, we have to accept the way it is.

The good news, however, is that there is plenty of good news, too. If you work the system I've just shared with you, you'll get more than plenty. More often than not you'll get what you want. And those are pretty good odds — the best out there.

Goals. There's no telling what you can do when you get inspired by them. There's no telling what you can do when you believe in them. There's no telling what will happen to you when you act upon them. Just try this system for ninety days. Just try it! It may work even better for you than it has for me.

I wish that for you.

STRATEGY TWO

Seek Knowledge

Chapter 5

The Path to Wisdom

One of the fundamental strategies of living the good life is knowing what information you need in order to achieve your aims. And once you know *what* you need to know, it's also helpful to know *how* to go about gathering that knowledge.

One of the best things Mr. Shoaff did for me in those early days was to instill in me the value of study.

He said, "If you wish to be successful, study success. If you wish to be happy, study happiness. If you want to make money, study the acquisition of wealth. Those who achieve these things don't do it by accident. It's a matter of studying first and practicing second."

Would you like to guess how many people make wealth a study? Right, very few. Considering the many men and women who seek wealth and happiness, you'd think they would make a careful study of them, don't you agree? Why they don't is yet *another* in that special category I call "mysteries of life."

Many years ago I learned that some of the best advice ever given comes from the Bible. There's a phrase in this amazing book that says, "If you search, you shall find." So *that* is the way to discover new knowledge that creates new ideas. Search. In order to find something, you must first search. Need a great idea to change your life? Rarely will it come out of nowhere. But if you make a diligent search for the knowledge you need, the right idea will come your way, often when you least expect it.

★ CAPTURING THE TREASURES OF KNOWLEDGE ★

Here is another fundamental word for you to ponder: capture. Great ideas pass by quickly and are easily forgotten . . . as can be true of those moments that make life worth living. That's why it's so important to learn to capture those things that really matter.

First, learn to capture special moments. Use a camera. Take lots of pictures. Being able to capture an event in a fraction of a second is a twentieth-century phenomenon. And how easy it is to take phenomena for granted!

Let me tell you about a recent experience. Over the past three years I've been invited to lecture annually in Taiwan. On my most recent trip to give a weekend seminar, there were about a thousand people in attendance. Now, if there were one thousand people in attendance, guess how many cameras were also in the room? Right — one thousand! Everyone brought a camera to capture the moments, the new friends, the new experiences. I ended up spending a big part of my time there posing for pictures.

Have you ever looked at the pictures of a few generations ago? Unfortunately there are relatively few still in circulation. But wouldn't it be wonderful if, instead, we had enough pictures to tell the whole story of what life was really like a hundred years ago? So don't be lackadaisical. Make sure you leave behind *your* whole story through a treasury of photographs and videos.

Another way to capture knowledge is in your own personal library. I don't mean the books your interior designer bought because they match with the blue decor. I mean those books that are dog-eared and well-marked — the ones you chose to study and underline; books with notes written in the margins; books that helped shape your philosophy of life values. *That* is truly a treasure worth capturing!

Today, with our expanded concept of communication, I'd also include in this treasure all the cassette tapes and videotapes that are shaping our lives for the better. That, too, is a special legacy to our children.

Finally, you'll want to capture all the knowledge you gain as you live your life. That's why I encourage you, as a serious student of wealth and happiness, to make use of a journal or diary as a gathering place for all the ideas that come your way. What will gradually emerge is an incredible treasure — business ideas, social ideas, cultural ideas, investment ideas, lifestyle ideas. Can you imagine the value in this? Certainly this kind of treasure is a more valuable heirloom than your old clock!

★ HOW TO GAIN WISDOM ★

There are two ways to gather wisdom. One way is to learn from your own life. The second is to study the lives of others.

Personal Reflection

Go over your life experiences. Learn the skill of reflection, which is the act of pondering life's events with the intent of learning from them. I call this process "rerunning the tapes."

The events of your life are some of the best sources of information. So don't merely *go* through your days — *get* from your days. Be aware of what's going on around you so that you'll drive the grooves in the record of the day deep into your consciousness.

There is a time and a place for everything. There are times to act and times to reflect. Most of us don't take the time for serious reflection. With our busy schedules we often neglect this crucial part of the formula for success.

At the end of the day take a few moments to review the happenings of the day — where you went, what you did, what you said. Ponder what worked and what didn't, what you want to repeat and what you want to avoid. Try to remember incidents as vividly as possible. Remember the colors, the sights, the sounds, the conversations, the experiences.

You see, experience can become commodity, currency, coin — an incredible source of value. But it can become all those things only if you take the time to record the experience, to ponder it, and then *turn* it into something of value. After all, it's not what happens to a person that makes the difference in how his or her life turns out. Rather, it's what he or she does with what happens that determines the outcome. And to do something positive about life, we must glean valuable information from it.

Another good time to reflect is at the end of major periods such as a week, a month, or a year. At the end of the week take a few hours for reflection to ponder the events of the past seven days. At the end of a month take a day. And at the end of a year take a week . . . to review, ponder, and reflect on everything that has happened in your life.

Sophisticated people have learned how to gather up the past and invest it in the future. When my father turned seventy-six I said to him, "Dad, can you imagine what it's going to be like to gather up the last seventy-five years and invest them in your seventy-sixth!"

Have you ever thought of life this way? That's how it can become productive and ever-exciting. Don't just live another year. Instead, gather up the years and *invest* them in the next one. Don't just have another conversation. Instead, gather up all your past conversations and invest them in your next one.

So start up a new discipline. Find out, by observing your life, what and how things work in this world. Never let it be said that you lived life without finding out about it. You may not be able to do all you find out, but make sure you find out all you can do. You don't want to live your life only to find that, ultimately, you lived only one-tenth of it, that you let the other nine-tenths go down the drain.

In studying your life, be sure to study the negatives as well as the positives, your failures as well as your successes. Our so-called failures serve us well when they teach us valuable lessons. Often, they're better teachers than our successes.

One of the ways we learn to do something right is by doing it wrong. Doing things wrong is a valuable course in life. Now, I would suggest that you not take this course for *too* long. If you've been doing something the wrong way for the past ten years, I wouldn't recommend another ten. But if you can learn quickly, there is no better, more emotionally effective way to learn than from personal experience.

When I met Mr. Shoaff I'd been working for six years. Shortly after we met he asked me, "Jim, how long have you been working now?" I told him.

"How are you doing?" he inquired further.

"Not very well," I said, a bit annoyed at having to admit this.

"Then I suggest you not do that anymore," he replied. "Six years is long enough to operate the wrong plan."

Then he asked, "How much money have you saved in the past six years?"

"None," I admitted sheepishly.

Raising his eyebrows, he said, "*Who* sold you on *that* plan?"

What a fantastic question. Where *did* I get this disastrous plan? Hey, everyone has bought *someone's* plan. The question is, *whose*?

WHOSE PLAN HAVE YOU BOUGHT?

Now, I must tell you that those initial confrontations with your own past experiences will be painful. This is especially true if you've made as many mistakes as I have. But think of the pay-off! Think of the progress you can make when you finally confront those errors!

Learning from Others

Another way you can gain knowledge is vicariously, through other people's experiences. And you can learn from other people's successes as well as from their failures. One of the reasons the Bible is such a good teacher is because it's a collection of human stories on both sides of the ledger.

One list of stories is called "examples." The message is: Do what these people did. The other list of stories is called "warnings." The message is: Don't do what these fools did. What a wealth of information!

But perhaps there is even another message. If your story ever gets into somebody's book, make sure it's used as an example, not as a warning . . .

There are three ways one can go about learning from others:

1. Through published literature such as books and audio tapes or videotapes.

2. By listening to the wisdom and folly of others.

3. Through observations of winners and losers.

Let's discuss each of these areas one by one:

Books and Tapes

All the successful people with whom I have had contact are good readers. They read, read, read. It's their curiosity that drives them to read. They simply *have* to know. They constantly seek new ways to become better. Here is a good phrase to remember: ALL LEADERS ARE READERS.

There used to be a time when publishing always referred to printed matter, such as books. But today we can learn through the miracle of electronic publishing as well. I'm referring to audio tapes and videotapes, both of which are excellent ways to acquire knowledge.

Many of the busiest people I know use audio cassettes to learn during unproductive times. For example, they often listen to tapes while driving in their cars. Listening to cassettes is an easy way to pick up innovative ideas and new skills.

Did you know there are thousands of books and tapes on how to be stronger, more decisive, a better speaker, a more effective leader, a better lover; develop influence; find a mate; become more sophisticated; start a business — and thousands of other useful topics? And yet many people do not use this wealth of knowledge. How do you explain that?

Did you further know that thousands of successful people have committed their inspiring stories to paper? And yet people don't want to read. How would you explain *that*?

Our "guy" is busy, I guess. He says, "Well, yeah. But you work where I work, by the time you struggle home it's late. You've got to have a bite to eat, watch a little TV to relax, and go to bed. You can't stay up half the night and read, *read*, READ." And this is the guy who is behind on his bills. He's a good worker, a hard worker, a *sincere* worker. Hey, you can be sincere and work hard all your life and still wind up broke, confused, *and* embarrassed. You've got to be better than a good worker. You've got to be a good reader. And if you don't like to read, at least you can listen to a good cassette on the way home, right?

Now you don't have to read books or listen to tapes half the night (although if you're broke, it's not such a bad idea). All I ask is that you devote just thirty minutes a day to learning. That's all.

You want to *really* do well? Then stretch your thirty minutes to a full hour. But at least spend thirty minutes. Oh yes, here's one more thing: Don't miss. Miss a meal, but not your thirty minutes of learning. All of us can afford to miss a few meals, but none of us can afford to lose out on ideas, examples, and inspiration.

The Bible teaches us that humans cannot live on bread alone. It tells us that next to food, our minds and souls must be nourished by words. Unfortunately, most people suffer from mental malnutrition.

Recently I told my staff, "Some people read so little that they have rickets of the mind." Not only should you feed your mind, you should make sure you have a well-balanced mental diet. Don't just feed your mind the easy stuff. You can't live on mental candy.

Think of your reading time as "tapping the treasure of ideas" time. And if somebody's got a good excuse for not tapping the treasure of ideas for at least thirty minutes every day or not investing some money on the acquisition of knowledge, then I'd like to hear it. Some excuses you *would not* believe! . . .

I say, "John, I've got this gold mine. I've got so much gold I don't know what to do with it all. Come on over and dig."

John says, "But I don't have a shovel."

"Well, John, go out and get you one."

He says, "Do you know what they're asking for shovels these days?"

Hey, invest the money. Get the books and tapes you need for your self-education. Don't shortchange yourself when it comes to investing in your own better future.

Mr. Shoaff got me started on books from the beginning. He said, "Become self-educated. Standard education will bring you standard results. Check the income figures of those with a standard education and see if that's what you want. If it isn't, if you want more than the average, you must become self-educated." So I went to work on building a library. And today I have one of the best.

Mr. Shoaff recommended a couple of books to get me started. One was the Bible, which I already had. It consists of sixty-six books and my parents saw to it that I was well-acquainted with them, so I figured I had a pretty good start.

But he also insisted that I get *Think and Grow Rich* by Napoleon Hill. If you haven't yet read it, I suggest you run right out and get a copy.

I must have read this great book several dozen times. I needed to. Mr. Shoaff said, "Repetition is the mother of skill." And the way my bank account was, I needed *lots* of skill.

As I look back, the information in the book has been worth tens of thousands of dollars to me. And yet I bought it for pennies. This taught me a powerful lesson: THERE CAN BE A GREAT DEAL OF DIFFERENCE BETWEEN COST AND VALUE. Before I met Mr. Shoaff, I used to ask, "How much does it cost?" But he taught me to ask, "What is it worth?" When I started to base my life on value instead of price, all kinds of things began to happen.

Remember: YOU ARE WHAT YOU READ.

One of the first things I do when I visit someone is to look through his or her library. I find out more by looking through someone's book and tape collection than I do through idle conversation.

Mostly, a library, or lack of one, tells me what a person is thinking or if he or she is thinking at all. The choice of books and tapes reveals a person's predominant thoughts, desires, and values.

What does your library say about you? You see, reading books is not some leisure-time luxury; it's a necessity for those who want to grow. So don't be like some of my friends who thought that graduating from high school or college gave them license to never read a book again. Start reading. And especially read the kinds of books that will help you to unleash your inner potential.

Are you now thinking about all the books you should read? Then here's some good news: You don't have to read all these books at once. Try reading two books a week. And if that seems like a lot, choose two thin books to start with. Do this for ten years and you'll end up reading over one thousand books! Do you think that acquiring the knowledge inside a thousand books will influence the many dimensions of your life? Of course it will.

Now it's also true that if you haven't been reading two books a week for the last ten years, you are a thousand books behind those who have. Are you beginning to understand the incredible disadvantage you'll have in ten years if you stride into the marketplace two thousand books behind? Why, for some of the more sophisticated confrontations you will serve as cannon fodder. They will chew you up and spit you out.

But that's not all. You'll also miss out on some terrific opportunities because of lack of knowledge. And your philosophy will be too shallow to sustain you through life's hardships.

Missing skills, missing knowledge, missing insight, missing values, missing lifestyle are all a result of not reading books. Remember, the book unread is the one that can't help you. You can't read too many books but you *can* read too few.

Listening

Listening is a wonderful way to learn. Let me propose to you an outrageous idea: Choose a really successful person and take him or her out to dinner. A poor person (and we're all poor compared to *someone*, no matter how well we're doing) should invest in feeding a rich person. And then do what? That's right — *listen*.

Go ahead, try it. Spend fifty, sixty, eighty, even a hundred dollars. Go for the full nine courses. Start with the hors d'oeuvres, and ask questions. Eat the salad (it will take about fifteen minutes) and keep the conversation going. The biggest steak in town will take forty-five minutes to demolish — keep asking questions. Order dessert. See how long you can stretch the meal. Try for at least two hours. If you get someone like this to talk with you for two hours, you can learn enough strategies and attitudes to multiply your income and change your life.

But of course you're right. Poor people don't take rich people out to dinner. That's probably why they're poor.

The "guy" says, "If he's rich, let him buy his own darn dinner! I'm not coming up with any money. And besides, if you work where I work, by the time you struggle home, it's late. You've got to have a bite to eat, watch a little TV to relax, and get to bed. You can't spend all that time trying to find a rich man to feed." And this man is behind on his payments. Behind! He's a good worker, a hard worker, a *sincere* worker. But you can work hard and be sincere all your life and still wind up broke and unhappy. You've got to be better than a good worker. You've got to be a good *listener*.

Observing

The third way to learn from others is to observe. Watch what successful people do. Why? Because success leaves clues. Watch how the successful man shakes the hand of someone else. Watch how the successful woman asks questions. People who do well *own* the habits of success. They create patterns of winning behavior just as the straggler creates patterns of losing behavior. You want to be promoted? Observe your superiors. Want to make as much money as your uncle? Observe how he manages his money and his lifestyle.

One of the reasons it's a good idea to attend seminars given by successful people is because you can observe them. No book or cassette, no matter how good, can convey the silent power of non-verbal communication. This is why videocassettes are becoming wonderful tools for total communication.

So become a good observer. Don't miss any clue that can help you change your life for the better.

★ INVESTING IN THE FUTURE ★

The search for knowledge is one of the strategies for wealth and happiness. What a powerful thought, to spend time in a consistent, disciplined, purposeful search for knowledge.

But as with everything else that's worthwhile, there's a price to pay. And this, unfortunately, stops some dead in their tracks. The search for knowledge involves making an investment. In fact, there are three kinds of investments it will take for you to successfully embark on this journey:

First, it will take the expenditure of money. It does take some money to purchase books and cassettes and to attend seminars. That's why I recommend you set up your own educational fund.

Each month, set aside a portion of your income and invest it in your search for knowledge. Spend the money to cultivate the sleeping giant inside you. The money — that's a small price. The promise is unlimited potential.

More important than money is your next expenditure: time. Time is a major expenditure. I understand that. It's one thing to ask a person to spend money, but it's an entirely different thing to ask him for his time.

Alas, there are no shortcuts. Until such time that a machine can be hooked up to pour knowledge into the brain, it will take time — precious time.

Fortunately, life has a unique way of rewarding high investment with high return. The investment of time you make now may be the catalyst for major accomplishment.

Finally, you'll be making an investment of effort. There is a great deal more effort involved in serious learning than in casual learning. In everything you do, be it self-observation, reading, or observing others, the intensity of your efforts will have a profound effect on the amount of knowledge you gain.

A focused mind is like a mental rifle shot that strikes an idea target. And to be that focused takes much concentrated effort. But it is precisely this effort that will open the floodgates to the place where great ideas can work their special magic to bring you closer to wealth and happiness.

STRATEGY THREE

Learn How to Change

Chapter 6

The Miracle of Personal Development

One day Mr. Shoaff said, "Jim, if you want to be wealthy and happy, learn this lesson well: Learn to work harder on yourself than you do on your job."

Since that time I've been working on my own personal development. And I must admit that this has been the most challenging assignment of all. This business of personal development lasts a lifetime.

You see, what you become is far more important than what you get. The important question to ask on the job is not, "What am I getting?" Instead, you should ask, "What am I becoming?" Getting and becoming are like Siamese twins: What you become directly influences what you get. Think of it this way: Most of what you have today you have attracted by becoming the person you are today.

So here's the great axiom of life: TO HAVE MORE THAN YOU'VE GOT, BECOME MORE THAN YOU ARE. This is where you should focus most of your attention. Otherwise, you just might have to contend with the axiom of *not* changing, which is: UNLESS YOU CHANGE HOW YOU ARE, YOU'LL ALWAYS HAVE WHAT YOU'VE GOT.

Income rarely exceeds personal development. Sometimes income takes a lucky jump, but unless you learn to handle the responsibilities that come with it, it will usually shrink back to the amount you can handle.

If someone hands you a million dollars, you'd better hurry up and *become* a millionaire. A very rich man once said, "If you took all the money in the world and divided it equally among everybody, it would soon be back in the same pockets it was before."

IT'S HARD TO KEEP THAT WHICH HAS NOT BEEN OBTAINED THROUGH PERSONAL DEVELOPMENT.

★ VALUE ★

In my early days there were several things that used to puzzle me. I used to wonder, "Why would one person be paid two thousand dollars a month and another be paid four thousand a month when they both work for the same company, handle the same product, work the same number of years, and come from the same background?"

What a puzzle! Why would one person do twice as well economically? In the area of compensation, what's the difference between two thousand and four thousand a month? (And don't tell me "two thousand dollars." That kind of difference I could've figured out even back then.)

"It must be a matter of time," I thought. "Some people do much better because they have more time. Mary ought to do well. She's got a lot of time. If I had all of Mary's time, I could also do well." Now that's got to be dumb, right? You can't get someone else's time . . .

A man once said to me, "If I had some extra time, I would make some extra money." I said, "Then you'll have to forget it. There isn't any more time. Where would you find any?"

Listen, my friend, when the clock strikes midnight, that's it! It's all over. There isn't any more time. And if you insist on finding more than twenty-four hours in one day, they'll come and take you away.

So if you can't create more time, what could you create that would make the difference in economic results? The answer is *value*. Value makes the difference. You can never create more time, but you can become more valuable.

This concept of value is a primary lesson in economics. Whether you work on the assembly line or sell goods or services, you get paid for the value. Now I know that you'll spend time bringing value to the marketplace. But you don't get paid for the *time*, you get paid for the *value*, for your productivity.

Mistakenly, the "guy" says, "I make twenty dollars an hour." That's not true! If it were true, he could just stay home and have them send over the money. No, he doesn't get paid twenty dollars for the *hour*. He gets paid twenty dollars for the *value* which has been placed on the hour he works. Paying by the hour is simply a convenient way to measure anticipated value.

That's why it's important to ask, "Is it possible to become twice as valuable and make twice as much money per hour? Is there a way for me to become three times or even four times more valuable within the same hour?" And the answer is, "Of course!" You *can* become more valuable *if* . . . (And there is always an if, right? Life is known as the "Big If." Harry Truman once said, "Life is 'iffy.' ") *if* you go to work primarily on yourself.

You see, it's easy to get "faked out." The "guy" says, "I've got ten years' experience. I don't know why I'm not doing better." What he hasn't realized is that he *doesn't* have ten years' experience. What he has is one year's experience repeated ten times. He hasn't made a single improvement, a single innovation in nine years!

Everybody wants more money. But most people look for it in the wrong places. Our "guy" says, "I need more money.

I'm going to work on my boss." Hey, I've found that bosses are notorious for not playing fast and loose with the company's till. I've never seen a boss get suddenly excited and for no reason triple somebody's wages.

Some people say, "We'll strike for more." The problem is that once you start striking you'll almost always have to strike the next time the contract is up. Besides, by demanding, all you'll get will be little bitty pieces — barely enough to get by. Forget the methods that will only help you to *barely* get by.

Listen, you can get by with a crust of bread and a pair of shoes. But that's not for you. You aren't reading this book to get the crumbs that fall off life's table. You want the feast, right?

I know some salespeople who always look for the angles. They say, "We'll get some of those sales books that teach the tricky sales. We'll lay it on the prospects, dazzle them with the sizzle, and grab their money before they know what happened to them." Well, I guess you can try that. But my experience shows that unless you give fair value, you'll wind up at the bottom of the economic ladder.

It's not what you get by tricks that counts. It's not what you get by demanding that counts. It's what you get by productive performance that counts.

I used to think that performance came from outside reasons. But I found out that real performance comes from those who have the right stuff inside them. I always looked for the answers outside. Then I learned that success and happiness are not values to pursue; they are values to develop.

People often ask me, "How do I develop an above-average income?" The answer is, become an above-average person. How?

For starters, develop an above-average handshake. Some people who say they want to succeed don't even work on their handshake. As easy as it would be to improve, they let it slide. They don't understand. Do you want to be above-average?

Then develop an above-average smile; develop an above-average interest in others; develop an above-average intensity to win. *That* will change everything.

There is nothing more pointless than looking for an above-average job with above-average pay without becoming an above-average performer. I call this *frustration*.

I used to say, "I sure hope things will change." That seemed my only hope. If conditions weren't going to change I was in serious trouble. Then I found out *nothing* was going to change, and I felt like I was drowning.

Not long ago I did a seminar in Honolulu for a group of oil company executives. We were sitting around a huge corporate table flanked with top executives from all over the world when one of them said, "Mr. Rohn, you know some important people around the world. What do you think the next ten years will bring?"

I said, "Gentleman, I *do* know the right people. I can tell you *exactly* what's going to happen." When I said that the room became very quiet. I continued, "Based on the people I know, and based on my life's experience, I've concluded that in the coming ten years it's going to be like it's always been." (Now aren't you glad I'm sharing this with you? It's not *everyone* who get's to hear this.)

I must admit that I said this to take some of the air out of this pompous group of big shots. But I also said it because it's absolutely true!

The tide comes in, and then what? That's right . . . it goes out. It's been that way for at least six thousand years of recorded history, and probably for much longer than that. It gets light and then what? It turns dark . . . That's the way it's been for at least six thousand years. We are not to be startled by this anymore.

If, when the sun goes down, a man says, "What happened, what happened?" we'd surely know that he just got here, right?

71

The next season after fall is . . . right again. And pray tell, how often does winter follow fall? *Every time, without fail . . .* for at least six thousand years.

True, some winters are long and some are short; some are difficult and some are easy. But no matter what, they always come after fall. *It isn't going to change.*

Sometimes you can figure it out, sometimes it's a puzzle. Sometimes it goes well, sometimes it's a disaster. Sometimes it sails along, sometimes it gets all tied up in knots. You see, it's not going to change. After six thousand years of recorded history, life is a mixture of opportunity and difficulty. That's the way it is.

The "guy" says, "Well then, how will my life change?" And the answer is, "Your life will change only when *you* change."

Whenever I speak, whether I address business executives or high school kids, my message is always the same: "The only way it gets better for you is when *you* get better." BETTER IS NOT SOMETHING YOU WISH; IT'S SOMETHING YOU BECOME.

★ THE SEASONS OF LIFE ★

Here are two phrases I want you to consider: The first is, "Life and commerce are like the seasons." The second is, "You cannot change the seasons but you *can* change yourself."

Now, with these two phrases as guides, let's take a look at the seasons of life and how you can best handle them:

Winter: A Time to Grow Strong

First and foremost, learn how to handle winters. There are all kinds of winters. There are economic winters, when the financial wolves are at the door; there are physical winters, when our health is shot; there are personal winters, when our heart is smashed to pieces. Wintertime. Disappointments. Loneliness. That's how the Blues were written.

So the big question is how do we handle the winters. Some people go to the calendar, tear out the month of January, and pretend it isn't there. But that's the childish approach. It solves nothing.

Let me tell you what mature people do: They get stronger. They get wiser. They get better.

Not a bad idea — to use the winter for personal development.

Before I understood this, I used to spend my winters looking for summers. I didn't understand.

Then, finally, when I was going through a sales slump, Mr. Shoaff said, "Don't wish it were easier, wish you were better. Don't wish for fewer problems, wish for more skills. Don't wish for less of a challenge, wish for more wisdom." Since then I can't honestly tell you that I've welcomed the winters, but I can tell you that I've used them to gear up for spring, which *always* comes after winter.

Spring: A Time to Take Advantage

Learn to take advantage of spring. What a great place for spring to be, right after winter. Opportunity follows difficulty. Expansion follows recession — just like clockwork. God is a genius.

Spring is the time to take advantage. Make a note of these two words. TAKE ADVANTAGE. Don't let the balmy weather confuse you. If you want to look good in the fall, this is the time to plant the seeds. In fact, we all have to excel at one of two things. Either we become good at planting in the spring or we learn how to beg in the fall.

So get busy in the spring. There is just a handful of springs for each of us. The Beatles wrote, "Life is so short." And for John Lennon on the streets of New York, life was extra short.

Summer: A Time to Take Care

Learn to nourish and protect your crops all summer. You can bet that as soon as you've planted, the insects and weeds will try to destroy your crop. And they will succeed, unless you prevent them.

Part of succeeding is learning to protect what you've created. And that's the greatest lesson of summer.

Here are two truths you'll learn during your summers:

First, you'll learn that all good will be attacked. Don't press me for the reason. I don't know why. But I do know that it's true. Every garden will be invaded. Not to understand this is naive.

Second, you'll learn that all values must be defended. *All* values — social, political, marital, commercial — must be defended. Every garden must be tended all summer. Unless you defend what you believe in, come fall you'll have nothing left.

Fall: A Time to Take Responsibility

Fall is the season where we reap the results of our springs and summers. Maturity can be defined by our ability to take full responsibility for the crops we have tended, either bountiful or meager.

Accepting full responsibility is one of the highest forms of human maturity — and one of the hardest. It's the day you pass from childhood to adulthood.

Learn to welcome fall without apology or complaint —

without apology if you've done well and without complaint if you've not. It's not easy, but it's the mature thing to do.

I used to have a lot of problems in this area, back in those early days. Just in case anyone asked, I used to carry with me a list of the reasons I wasn't doing well. My list, which I predictably called "reasons for not doing well" included lots of alibis.

I blamed the government. The government was at the top of my list.

I blamed taxes. "Look what you've got left after they take everything out."

I blamed prices. "You walk into a supermarket with twenty dollars and come out with half a bag of groceries."

I blamed the weather.

I blamed the traffic.

I blamed my car and the car manufacturer.

I blamed my negative relatives: "They are always putting me down."

I blamed my cynical neighbors.

I blamed the community.

Hey, I had lots of good reasons for not doing well. At least I thought I did.

Mr. Shoaff was very kind, but he was also blunt. One day he looked up at me and with a quizzical expression on his face asked, "Jim, just out of curiosity, tell me why you haven't done well up to now." Excellent question, right?

Well, so that I wouldn't look bad, I decided to run through my list. How I ever had the nerve I'll never know, but I did.

I went through the whole litany — the government, taxes, prices — everything. He listened patiently as I went through it all. When I was finished he peered at my list for a few moments. Finally, shaking his head, he said, "There's only one thing wrong with your list . . . *You* ain't on it."

Afterward, I quickly tore up my list of "reasons for not doing well." Then I got a fresh piece of paper and put one word across the top: "Me."

There's a Negro spiritual that says it all: "It's not my mother nor my father nor my brother nor my sister, but it's me, Oh Lord, standin' in the need of prayer." I used to blame everything outside me for my lack of progress until I found that my problem was inside.

It's not what happens that determines the outcome. What happens, happens. And it happens to everybody.

Two brothers have an abusive, alcoholic father. One becomes a criminal, the other a judge. The same event — different results. How can that be? It's because it's not what happens but rather what you and I do about it that matters. Anything can happen, right? I've heard all the stories; I've *been* one of these stories. We could all tell war stories for days on end . . .

Have you heard of Murphy's Law? Murphy has this law that says, "If anything can go wrong, it will." And it does! I, too, have fallen out of the sky many times — once, to the tune of two million dollars. Devastating! (It took me a while to get over that one.)

Now I admit that to some people a couple of "mill" isn't all that much. But it was *all* I had. That's a lot, any time you lose all you've got. There was a time when once you ran out of money and got to zero you were through. Heck, today they'll let you whistle by zero on borrowed money. These days they'll bury you with credit.

But those are happenings . . .

Everyone's got his or her story. Someone says, "Yes, but you don't understand the disappointments I've had." Come on! Everyone has disappointments. Disappointments are not special gifts reserved for you. The question is, what are *you* going to do about them?

★ SELF-IMPOSED LIMITATIONS ★

To be successful we must all work to eliminate those self-imposed limitations that are stunting our personal development. And no matter who you are, there are three self-imposed limitations you have to contend with. Let me tell you about them.

The first limitation is procrastination. Procrastination is especially dangerous because of its accumulating nature: When we put off doing some minor task, it doesn't seem to be all that important. And if we let a few things slide during the day, it doesn't seem like such a bad day. But let enough of those days pile up and you have the makings of a disastrous year.

Blame is another self-imposed limitation. At one time or another all of us have blamed someone for something. We have had long training in this self-imposed limitation going back to a certain fruit garden where the man said, "It was the woman. She got me into this." And the woman blamed the serpent.

Why do we point fingers instead of looking within? The ego strives to defend itself. Therefore, when we blame outside forces we don't have to face our own weaknesses and failings. This must have been my reason for keeping my infamous "list of reasons."

One of my favorite items on the list was the high cost of everything. One day, after some inane statement I made about the cost of an item, Mr. Shoaff cut me short. "Listen, Jim," he said, "cost is not your problem. It's not that *it* costs too much. The problem is that *you* can't afford *it*." And he was right.

It's never the fault of *it*. If you keep shifting responsibility to *it* you'll always be broke and disillusioned. You'll never earn enough. But when you start thinking in terms of "me" instead of "it" you'll experience a surge of personal growth and income.

Excuses, the third self-imposed limitation, is a close relative of blame. Guess how many excuses exist? Right, millions! And people create a million more in the course of their lives. In fact, people go to tremendous lengths to avoid facing the truth — which is that *they* are responsible. I guess they'd rather create a million excuses than create a million dollars. (You can't have both.)

So here is the fundamental question you must answer: What are you going to do, starting *today*, to improve yourself? It really boils down to this: If you don't get rid of some of your own self-imposed limitations, the next five years will be about the same as the last, except that you'll be five years older. But by taking responsibility and getting rid of your self-imposed limitations, you can, instead, become five years better. Now, doesn't *this* sound more exciting?

There are many who have little faith in their own ability. They ask themselves, "What am I *capable* of doing? What can I do to make a difference in how my life turns out?"

Let me first give you the broad answer to these questions. *You* can do the most remarkable things, no matter what kinds of winters life throws your way. People can rise to unbelievable heights when called upon: A woman lifts a two-ton car to save her child; a man survives starvation and disease in a concentration camp because he dreams of seeing his family; immigrants start their new lives by washing dishes and within five years, by scrimping and saving, own their own thriving businesses with scores of native-born on their payroll. Remarkable!

I also found out that kids can do remarkable things — that is if they have remarkable things to do. Just get them away from the TV and challenge their minds and bodies; they will grow to be remarkable people. (I've also discovered that if they don't have remarkable things to do, there's no telling *what* they will do. But that's another matter . . .)

Human beings can do remarkable things because they are remarkable. You and I aren't amoeba, fish, birds, or dogs. We can turn nothing into something, pennies into fortune, disaster into triumph. In contrast, when a dog starts with weeds he ends up with weeds. The reason? He's just a dog. He doesn't have the ability to create.

So accept the fact that you are remarkable. Thrive on your uniqueness! Reach down inside yourself and bring out more of your remarkably human gifts. They are there, waiting to be discovered and used.

Once you bring out all your gifts, you can change anything you need to change:

If you don't like how it is for you now, change it.

If it isn't enough, change it.

If it doesn't suit you, change it.

If it doesn't please you, change it.

Remember: YOU CAN CHANGE ALL THINGS FOR THE BETTER WHEN YOU CHANGE YOURSELF FOR THE BETTER. After all, you aren't just a plant or an animal, completely dependent on instinctive behavior. You are a human being, a most remarkable creation.

You and I are too sophisticated to think that we can change simply by reading this bit of philosophical insight. It will take lots more than that. What *will* it take? Perhaps I should first tell you what *isn't* going to do it . . .

Some people will tell you: "Enthusiasm makes all the difference." We hear a lot about enthusiasm these days. The old cliche perseveres. In the typical sales meeting one still hears it being chanted in staccato unison by a chorus of bleary-eyed salespeople:

"To.be.en.thu.si.as.tic.you.must.feel.en.thu.si.as.tic."

But, you see, enthusiasm *by itself* won't help. I'm sorry. After you have leaped about, jumping and shouting, there are still some things waiting for you to do. And unless you do them, things simply won't change. A man can get all excited about lifting two-hundred-pound weights — until he gets to the gym. Then he needs a new kind of excitement, long-term excitement that will keep him in training until he *can* lift the two hundred pounds. We call this kind of excitement *discipline*.

Frankly, discipline is the only thing that will do it. It is the only vehicle for real progress. If there is one thing to get excited about, it's discipline. Get excited about your ability to do the necessary things for growth. That's true excitement, not just hopeful panic.

★ HOW TO CHANGE ★

No one understands as I do the inherent difficulty in changing old and persistent habits. But habits begin to change when we begin to change our perceptions.

Most of us don't experience a huge cataclysmic transformation. No, for most of us change comes as an evolutionary process of almost imperceptible changes. We just keep nudging ourselves in the right direction, forming one or two better habits here and there, until finally we realize we have turned around a major area of our life.

The Three Areas of Personal Development

In your quest for personal development, there are three areas for you to consider: You can look at developing yourself spiritually, physically, and mentally.

Spiritual Self-Development

I must confess that I consider myself an amateur in this

area. Because I was raised in a home filled with deep faith (my father is a preacher, a fact which makes me — for better or for worse — a PK, or preacher's kid), I was imbued with a love for God's creation. But regardless of your background (this book is written for people of all backgrounds and beliefs), I think you should evaluate what growth and change you want to make in this vital area. Spiritual and ethical values will help build a strong foundation underneath your quest for wealth and happiness.

Physical Self-Development

The Bible teaches that we should treat our bodies like temples. And, indeed, the Jewish laws for hygiene are elaborate and specific.

But beyond hygiene, I think we need to make a point of "draping our temple," dressing in a way that's appropriate to our desire to succeed.

Let's face it, how we appear to others does make a difference in terms of our ability to function well in the marketplace. In fact, there is another biblical phrase that tells us to take care of the outside for people and take care of the inside for God. People look on the outside, at least initially, and God looks on the inside, always.

Now maybe you think people *shouldn't* judge you by your personal appearance. Well let me tell you, they do! And because they do, you should make a point of looking your best. (There are lots of good books on this subject, so check with your bookstore or library.)

Another aspect of physical development has to do with staying in shape. The body and mind work together. And for your mind to have the stamina to strive, your body should be in as good a shape as possible.

Do you have a regular exercise program? If not, find one you can follow and get started. In addition, make sure you pay attention to the foods you eat and the supplemental nutrition you take.

Mental Self-Development

For most people mental development stops at an early age. Once they have a good job, it's easy for many to stop pursuing mental development.

Have you heard about the accelerated learning curve? From birth to age eighteen our learning curve is dramatic. We learn a staggering amount quickly, but as we grow older and find our niche in the marketplace, our learning curve reaches a plateau.

In the past, if all you wanted was an average life, this non-growth mentality was acceptable. I say *was* because that's no longer true. The last few decades of the twentieth century are demanding constant growth and learning.

As technology keeps accelerating the pace of change, no one can simply hold on to a job and expect that job to remain the same for forty years. The my-grandfather-used-to-work-here-my-father-works-here-and-now-I-work-here mentality is dying, killing with it the hopes of those who are not willing to accept the need to grow and to adapt.

On the positive side, can you imagine what you can become if you keep up an accelerated learning curve throughout your life? Can you imagine what skills you'll develop, what insights you'll have?

★ THE EASY WAY TO DISCIPLINE ★

Because forming the habit of personal growth will require the consistent effort that only discipline provides, let me give you a key to discipline.

Start with the little disciplines and begin to string them together. Gradually, you'll discover that by tackling many small disciplines you'll have mastered a big one.

I urge you to take on a small challenge, something you can do right now. And then take on another. After awhile, when the big challenges come your way you'll be able to handle them with complete confidence.

Do you want to lose weight? Start by eating your bread unbuttered.

Do you want to go to Europe? Start by setting aside twenty dollars each week.

Do you want to be punctual? Start by getting up a half hour earlier.

Do you want to make a million-dollar sale? Start by making a fifty-dollar sale.

As Robert Schuller says, "Inch by inch everything's a cinch." But if you never take the small steps, no one, including yourself, will trust you with the big ones. Don't be like the man who struts out of his house determined to straighten out the profit picture of the corporation when he hasn't even straightened out his own personal budget. Who is he kidding!

You see, everything affects everything else. Every discipline, or lack of one, affects every other discipline.

Mistakenly, a man says, "This is the only place where I let down." That cannot be! Every low standard will adversely affect the rest of your performance. Why? Because doing less than you are capable of doing creates lack of self-esteem. And lack of self-esteem is the greatest deterrent to success.

★ SELF-MOTIVATION ★

Recently I was on a lecture tour in Australia and was interviewed by the news media. They asked, "Mr. Rohn, are you one of those American motivators?" I said, "No, I'm a businessman. I can share my ideas and my experiences, but people have got to motivate themselves."

It took me a while, but I finally realized that you can't change others. Lord knows, I've tried.

Once I was managing a group of uninspired salespeople. Feeling challenged, I said, "I'm going to make them successful if it kills me." Guess what? I almost died.

Good people are found, not changed. Sure, *they* can change *themselves*, but you and I can't change them. People ask me, "How do I recruit good people?" and I answer, "You have to find good people." That's the best answer I can give.

Here is the first rule of successful management: DON'T SEND YOUR DUCKS TO EAGLE SCHOOL. Why? Because it won't work. All you'll get are unhappy ducks. They won't soar like eagles. They'll just quack, quack, quack. And then they'll "poop" on you. I know . . . I've tried.

Recently a full-page ad for a hotel chain caught my eye. The headline said, "We don't teach our people to be nice." Now *that* got my attention. And in smaller print the ad continued, "We simply hire nice people." Wow! What a clever shortcut!

Motivation is a mystery. Why does one salesperson see a first prospect at seven in the morning and another salesperson is just getting out of bed at eleven? I don't know. It's part of the mysteries of life.

I give a lecture to a thousand people. One walks out and says, "I'm going to change my life." Another walks out with a yawn, muttering to himself, "I've heard all this stuff before." Why is that? Why wouldn't both be affected the same way? Another mystery.

The millionaire says to a thousand people, "I read this book and it started me on the road to wealth." Guess how many go out and get the book? That's right . . . very few. Isn't it incredible? Why wouldn't *everyone* get the book? . . . a mystery of life.

Now, you've already got a lot going for you. Your reading this book proves that you've got the inner motivation to grow and to change. I urge you to build on this foundation to become all you're capable of being.

I know you will!

STRATEGY FOUR

*Control
Your
Finances*

Chapter 7

How to Achieve Financial Freedom

Money is an emotional topic, and most of us have ambivalent feelings about it. On one hand we want the security and comfort it can bring; on the other hand we fear financial success will somehow corrupt our ethics. Certainly, TV and movies do their parts to characterize wealthy people as scheming and evil. When was the last time you saw a program that depicted a rich person as the "good guy?"

In religious circles one often hears the Bible misquoted by well-meaning people. Instead of, "The *love* of money is the root of all evil," some people tell us that "*Money* is the root of all evil." Obviously, it is the complete quotation of the Bible which is correct. If you make money your love and you pursue affluence to the exclusion of or at the expense of other values, you have lost, not won.

However, let us consider this question: If you *could* do better, should you? Within the time you've allocated to gainful work, shouldn't you try to accomplish the most you can?

I believe the greatest satisfactions of life come to those of us who make a habit of doing the best with what we've got. In fact, doing less than our best has a way of weighing on our psyche.

We humans seem to be creatures of enterprise. We're challenged by the seasons. We see the soil and the sun and the rain and the seed and we feel them urging us to harness them. It's as if life and nature are saying, "Do you have the genius to make something unique of us? We are the raw materials. What splendid things can you create while you are here?"

You and I, as creatures of enterprise, shouldn't be reluctant to go for it — for high productivity, for the full employment of our genius, for the full development of our potential in all areas of our lives — including the area of creating wealth. That is the essence of life.

Sophisticated people know that it isn't the amount that matters; it's doing all that we can do with our God-given abilities that really counts.

This last thought — doing all that we can with what we have — is the essence of a special book. It's called, *The Richest Man in Babylon*, by George Clayson. It's a small book which can be read in one sitting, but it covers the basics. I call it, The Appetizer for the Full Discourse on the Subject of Financial Independence, and I recommend it to you.

Our actions and acquisitions say a great deal about us. They reveal our philosophy of life, our attitude, knowledge, and thoughts — even our character. Because the outer always reflects the inner, they provide a running commentary on our ability to weigh and to perceive.

There's even an adage that says, "What you do speaks so loudly, I can't hear what you're saying."

There's no escaping it: Everything is symptomatic of something. It's either symptomatic of something right or it's symptomatic of something wrong. That's why it's such a wise policy not to ignore symptoms. In case something in your life isn't working as it should, they act as an early-warning system, proclaiming to anyone willing to listen that something must change.

For example, you could take a look at your lifestyle in relation to your income. If you're spending more than you're making, you may be committing slow financial suicide. Your next "toy," purchased on the installment plan, could be no less than another dose of poison served to you on a silver platter.

Look at what you're doing with your present income. Are you using it in a wise manner, spending no more than seventy percent of your total income? Or are you living a few hundred or a few thousand dollars a month above your earnings? Take a look at the symptoms before it's too late.

I remember saying to Mr. Shoaff, "If I had more money I would have a better plan." He quickly answered, "I would suggest that if you had a better plan you would have more money." This is a statement of major importance! You see, it's not the *amount* that counts; it's the *plan* that counts. It's not how *much* you allocate but *how* you allocate it.

★ DIVIDING THE FINANCIAL PIE ★

When was the last time someone taught you how our economic system works? I don't mean in some theoretical textbook way but in terms of real-life, everyday economics? Has anyone ever told you the wisest way to allocate every dollar you earn? I certainly wasn't taught any of this until Mr. Shoaff patiently took me by the hand and explained it to me.

Real-life economics must be one of the most glaring omissions in our educational system. I say this because in my travels to lecture throughout the world, I constantly run into otherwise well-educated people — doctors, lawyers, top corporate personnel, even entrepreneurs — who haven't the vaguest notion as to how to manage their finances.

These otherwise sophisticated people may be able to read complex annual reports, but they don't seem to understand everyday economics, the economics of becoming financially independent on a steady, ongoing, ever-predictable basis.

As a result of their ignorance, they do not teach this basic economics to their children. And so, generation after generation remains ignorant of the miracle that is the free-enterprise system.

Indulge me, then, as I take time to review how money is to be allocated for the creation of wealth.

Taxes

I realize that the topic of taxes may seem like a strange place to begin the discussion of creating wealth. And yet throughout our lives, whether young or old, we must learn the necessity of paying taxes. And as soon as they have any money at all, our children, too, must learn that when they spend money they immediately become consumers. And all consumers of goods and services, no matter how young, must pay taxes.

If a child is only six years old when he first goes to the store to buy something that costs a dollar, the proprietor will ask him for an additional six cents. The child may look at the price tag and ask the proprietor what the six cents is for. This is the time to offer a full explanation. If he's going to take six cents from the child, shouldn't the merchant tell him where it goes? After all, it's *his* six cents. The child might ask the proprietor who keeps it. The merchant would then explain that it's for taxes, that *he* doesn't get to keep it but merely collects it.

The next two obvious questions the child might ask are who gets it and what's it used for. And with these questions come very important answers. The child should be told that because we have all agreed to live together, we call ourselves a society. And for society to function properly, there are some things we cannot do for ourselves alone.

For example, we cannot each build a piece of the street. The machinery would be too expensive, and it would take too long to learn how to use it. So we have a government. And a government is made up of people who do things for us that we cannot or do not want to do ourselves. Because the streets, the sidewalks, the police, and the fire department must all be paid for, we've agreed to add some money each time we buy something and give it to the government.

Understanding this is important. Our children have to learn this. *We* have to learn this.

We then move on to federal taxes. Here is a good way to explain federal taxes. I call it The Care and Feeding of the Goose that Lays the Golden Eggs. It's so important to feed the goose — not to abuse the goose or tear off its wings — but to feed and care for it.

What's that you say? The goose eats too much? That's probably true. But then, don't we *all* eat too much? If so, let not one appetite accuse another. If you step on the scales and you're ten pounds too heavy, you've got to say, "Yes, the government and I are each about ten pounds too heavy. Looks like we both eat too much." No question about it. Every appetite must be disciplined — yours, mine, and the government's. Hey, we could *all* go on a diet!

Mr. Shoaff urged me to become a happy taxpayer. Now, I must admit it took a while, but I finally did become a happy taxpayer. Part of this transformation occurred when I began to understand the function of taxes and that it is right for everyone to pay his or her fair share.

I finally decided I didn't mind picking up my share of the tab for defense. It's so necessary for our safety as a country to keep the international bullies away. Some people say, "Why bother with all that expensive equipment? They won't come over here." Obviously, those people haven't been reading their history books.

Others say, "We're not about to pick up the tab for defense." Well then, I suggest they go to a place which doesn't offer defense as part of the package. If one is going to enjoy the benefits, one should pay a share.

Jesus, the master teacher, gave some clear advice when he said, "Pay Caesar first." That's pretty clear — pay Caesar first. For some reason, he didn't qualify this statement or take the time to criticize the government. All he said was, "Pay Caesar first." I don't think we need a prophet to interpret *that one* for us.

Now, before you go out and promptly fire your tax advisor, let me add this: Don't pay *more* than you should. By all means take advantage of the incentives. They were given to you as a reward for channeling your money into areas the government thinks help the economy.

All I'm saying is that when everything has been computed, all legitimate deductions have been taken, and you reach that last line on your income tax form, whatever the amount, pay it. And pay with happiness, knowing that you're feeding the goose that lays the golden eggs — the golden eggs of freedom, safety, justice, and free enterprise.

Some goose!

Some eggs!

Furthermore, I believe everyone should pay — even the poorest person. I don't care if it's just one dollar a year. That would be enough. The point is that everyone should *enjoy* the dignity of paying his or her fair share.

There is the story about Jesus and some of his disciples who were watching the people come to offer their contributions to the temple. Some came with large amounts. Others gave smaller amounts. Finally a little old woman came and carefully put two pennies in the treasury. Jesus pointed to the woman and said, "Look at this wonderful woman who gave her two pennies." The disciples were puzzled. "Two pennies!" they exclaimed. "Of all the magnificent donations given here today, why are you pointing to this poor woman as an example?"

Jesus said, "You don't understand, but she gave more than anyone else." They said, "Two pennies — more than anyone else? Explain that to us, Rabbi." He said, "Yes, for her the two pennies represented all she had."

How remarkable!

But let's examine this story further. Sometimes what is *not* told has a more profound lesson than what *is* told. Consider what Jesus did not do. He did not take the two pennies out of the treasury and return them to the old lady, saying, "Here, old woman, we have observed that you are so poor and so pitiful that we are going to give you back your two pennies." What an insult that would have been! She would surely have said, "What's the matter, aren't my two pennies good enough? They represent a considerable portion of what I own. Would you take away my dignity?" Of course, this scene did not occur. And therein lies the most profound lesson.

The 70/30 Rule

After you pay your fair share of taxes, you must learn to live on seventy percent of your after-tax income. This is important because of the way you'll allocate your remaining thirty percent. The seventy percent you will spend on necessities and luxuries. The thirty percent? Let's allocate it in the following ways:

Charity

Of the thirty percent not spent, one-third should go to charity. Charity is the act of giving back to the community that which you have received in order to help those who need assistance. I believe that contributing ten percent of your after-tax income is a good amount to strive for. (You may choose a larger or smaller amount — it's *your* plan.)

Some people like to give their charity through their church or community organization; others prefer to give it individually. But whether you administer it yourself or give your money to an institution to administer, be sure to set aside a percentage of your income for giving.

The act of giving should be taught early in life. The best time to teach a child the act of charity is when he gets his first dollar. Take him on a visual tour. Take him on a tour of a place where people are truly helpless so that he learns compassion. If a child understands, he won't have any trouble parting with a dime. Children have big hearts.

There is a reason why the act of giving should be taught when the amounts are small: It's pretty easy to take a dime out of a dollar. But it's considerably harder to give away a hundred thousand dollars out of a million. You say, "Oh, if I had a million I'd have no trouble giving a hundred thousand." I'm not so sure. A hundred thousand is a lot of money. We'd better start you early so you'll develop the habit before the big money comes your way.

Capital Investment

With your next ten percent of your after-tax income you're going to create wealth. This is money you'll use to buy, fix, manufacture, or sell. The key is to engage in commerce, even if only on a part-time basis.

I believe that everyone in this country should engage in some form of capitalism. Here, we believe that capital belongs in the hands of the people.

Communism, on the other hand, teaches that capital belongs in the hands of the state.

This makes for a great contrast. Communism has little trust in the ability of the individual to make wise decisions. Instead, those in power want to keep everything centralized, in the hands of the government. In our country, as in all other countries with free enterprise, we believe that the genius resides with the populace. It's the individual, not the state, who will come up with innovations for goods and services. The pursuit of profit is a powerful incentive to create a life of abundance for everyone.

So how do you go about creating wealth with the ten percent of your income you set aside for that purpose?

There are lots of ways. Let your imagination roam. Take a close look at those skills you developed at work or through your hobbies; you may be able to convert these into a profitable enterprise.

In addition, you can also learn to buy a product at wholesale and sell it for retail. Or you can purchase a piece of property and improve it. And if you're fortunate enough to work at a place where you're rewarded for additional productivity, you can work for more income and use this income to invest in an ownership position through the purchase of stocks.

Use this ten percent to purchase your equipment, products, or equity — and get started. There is no telling what genius lies sleeping inside you waiting to be awakened by the spark of opportunity.

Here is an exciting thought! Why not work full time on your job and part time on your fortune? Why not, indeed? And what a feeling you'll have when you can honestly say, "I'm working to become wealthy. I'm not just working to pay my bills." When you have a wealth plan, you'll be so motivated that you'll have a hard time going to bed at night.

Savings

The last ten percent should be allotted to savings. I consider this to be one of the most exciting parts of your wealth plan because it can offer you peace of mind by preparing you for the "winters" of life. And through the magic of compounding, greatly aided by the new tax-free retirement programs available to every working person in this country, you can accumulate a princely sum over the years.

Economics 101: A Child's View

The best time to teach capitalism is when a child discovers that he can make some extra money by making himself useful. But beyond giving them an allowance, you can show your kids how to enter the realm of true enterprise.

For example, kids ought to have two bicycles — one to ride and one to rent. This way they can begin to understand the world of commerce. It really doesn't take much to be in business; it doesn't take a million dollars. And what's exciting is that a child can learn the basic business principles of running a General Motors by operating a successful bicycle rental business.

Here's another idea. Show children how to buy a bottle of soap for two dollars and sell it for three dollars — right in the neighborhood. It's capitalism in action — profits, products, and services brought to the marketplace. It's the stuff of which fortunes are made.

And teach your child the advantage of being a child. Tell him that some people will buy from him just because he's a kid . . .

Johnny goes a few doors down from your home and knocks on Mrs. Jones' door. Mrs. Jones answers. Johnny says, "Mrs. Jones, I have this bottle of soap. It's the best there is. My mother uses it, and lots of people I know wouldn't use anything else. You should really have some. It only costs three dollars, and since I'm your neighbor, I can take care of you. And besides . . . I'm just a kid."

There, isn't that simple? Here is a small example of commerce in action, capitalism at its most basic level.

Mrs. Jones says, "Johnny, I appreciate your coming by. I think your product is good, but really, to be honest with you, I have lots of soap."

"Let me come in and check," says Johnny, charging forward. (Kids know how to overcome objections. They don't stand on ceremony.)

Mrs. Jones, knowing that her objections are useless, says, "Okay, I'll be a customer."

Johnny rushes home excited. He says, "I've got three dollars to spend."

"If you spend all three dollars," you remind him, "you'll be out of business."

"Oh," sighs Johnny, a bit disappointed. "I see what you mean."

You go on to explain, "First, you must set aside two dollars to invest in another bottle of soap. You must not spend your capital. Capital must be carefully preserved. What would you think of a farmer who ate his seed corn? Dumb farmer, right? So capital, which is known as seed money, must be defended. It's your only chance for another harvest."

Johnny can't argue with your explanation, so after considering the matter, he says, "Okay, I'll set aside the two dollars so I can stay in business and continue to make a one-dollar profit. But I do get to spend the dollar profit, don't I?"

Now comes your opportunity to show Johnny the difference between staying poor and becoming rich. You explain, "If you spend all your profit, you'll wind up broke and unhappy."

Johnny doesn't understand. So you take him to the poorest neighborhood in town and you ask him, "Do you want to live like this?"

"No."

"All right then. You can't spend the whole dollar."

"Then what do I do with it?"

"First, you must pay your taxes." And for kids this is easy.

They pay when they spend — unless they start making serious money, in which case you must teach them about federal taxes. (Remember the goose and its eggs?)

Next, you remind Johnny of the need for charity. Johnny remembers. "Oh yes, here is ten cents for those who cannot help themselves. Now can I spend the rest?"

"No, no," you reply. "You'll still wind up broke and just a little less unhappy."

"Okay, okay, what now?" Johnny is becoming impatient.

"The next ten cents out of your one-dollar profit is for the increase of your capital. If you keep setting aside ten cents for every dollar you make, you'll someday have enough to buy two bottles of soap instead of one."

"Oh, sure." Now Johnny is really catching on. "If I can buy two bottles instead of one, I save myself a trip and sell more bottles."

How clever!

Next, you explain that some companies will charge you less per bottle when you buy two. If they sell one bottle for two dollars, they might sell two bottles for three dollars and eighty cents. Johnny is excited. "Wow!" he exclaims. "When I sell it I can even make more profit!"

And it's true. Everybody benefits from the increase in capital. The company gets to sell two bottles at a time, Johnny saves a trip and some costs, and he can keep some of the savings or pass them on to Mrs. Jones as an incentive to buy two bottles instead of one.

Johnny says, "Hey, this is neat. Now do I get to spend the rest of my profit?"

"No, we still need to do one more thing. We're going to rent your money to the bank."

"How does that work?"

So you explain. "Out of your profit you need to take out ten cents and put it into a financial institution, like a bank. They are going to pay you a fee for renting your money. They call it interest."

"Why would a bank want to do this?"

"Because some projects, like building a tall building or a factory, take more capital than any individual has. So we have a system where all of us can invest our money in a bank so that the bank has enough money to lend for big projects. This helps create more jobs, and that helps everyone. In the meantime, the bank will pay you for the use of your money."

"What kind of interest do they pay kids?"

"The same as they pay adults."

Johnny has a hard time believing this. "You mean I get the interest of an adult when I'm only a kid?" he asks incredulously.

"That's right. Your money can grow as quickly as anyone else's."

"Can I get my money back?"

"Sure, and you'll always get more than you put in."

"Hey, that's pretty good. Now can I spend what's left?"

"Yes, Johnny, let's go out and have some ice cream."

I bet you probably knew all of this. But when I met Mr. Shoaff at age twenty-five, I was just as naive as Johnny. I wonder how many adults were never taught how they can have a wealth plan . . .

If you have children, be sure to explain to them the wealth plan. Show them that if they start using the 70/30 formula while they're young, they will become financially independent at age forty. They could, then, spend the rest of their lives doing only what they want to do.

Let me give you the definition of "rich" and "poor." Poor people spend their money and save what's left. Rich people save their money and spend what's left. It's the same amount of money — just a different philosophy.

Twenty years ago, two people each earned a thousand dollars a month and they each earned the same increases over the years. One had the philosophy of spending money and saving what's left; the other had the philosophy of saving first and spending what's left. Today, if you knew them both, you'd call one poor and the other wealthy.

But saving, like any form of discipline, has a subtle effect. At the end of a day, a week, or a month, the results are hardly noticeable. But let five years lapse, and the differences become pronounced. At the end of ten years, the differences are dramatic.

Here's a great philosophy that we can learn from a lowly member of the animal kingdom. It's called "the ant philosophy." You know the ants. There's a biblical phrase that urges everyone, especially lazy people, to study ants. Ants are unique for two reasons:

First, an ant will never quit. If it's headed somewhere and you put an obstacle in its way, it will either try to climb over it or go under or around it. If you remove the obstacle, away it goes. And if you put another obstacle in its way, the ant will look for a way — over, under, or around. How long will an ant keep trying? Until it dies. An ant will *never* quit.

What a lesson!

The second reason ants are unique? Guess what ants plan for all summer? That's right — winter. And how much will an ant gather in the summer to prepare for winter? *All* it can! How intelligent!

Do you remember the fable about the grasshopper? He laughed at the ant for storing grain all summer, while he kept leaping about the high grass without a care about the future. When the harsh winter came he starved to death while the ant had plenty.

Rich or poor — the difference is not so much in how much you make as it is in how you use what you make. The choice is yours.

★ MID-COURSE CORRECTIONS ★

What do you think of when you think of old people? Do you see people who are somewhat helpless and who live on limited resources? Indeed, this is the predominant condition of the majority of those who fall into the group known as "senior citizens."

Wouldn't it be wonderful if we could change that image? I've come up with a new definition of what grandparents ought to be. The major role of grandparents should be to teach their grandchildren how to be wealthy, cultured, and happy "just like us." Grandparents should not have to say, "I've worked all my life and now I need help." They should be able to say, "I've worked all my life; now I can help."

If you are not financially independent by age forty or fifty, it doesn't mean that you live in the wrong country. It doesn't mean that you live in the wrong community. Nor does it mean that you live in the wrong time or that you're the wrong person. It simply means that you have the wrong plan.

And you're far from being alone. Most of us get off course.

When they send a rocket to the moon, they know the rocket will eventually get a little off course. The first set of guidance systems will not be enough for the whole trip. There will be need for a mid-course correction.

You and I are no different. From time to time we, too, must execute our own mid-course correction if we are to become financially independent. After all, wouldn't you want to be the kind of grandparent who can serve as a role model for wealth and happiness?

★ KEEPING SCORE ★

Soon after I met him, Mr. Shoaff asked me if I have a financial statement. I asked, "What is a financial statement?"

Mr. Shoaff patiently explained that it's very important to know exactly where you are, without kidding yourself. Only when you know where you are can you possibly have a good plan for going forward to where you want to be.

It isn't hard to do. You merely list the value of your assets on one side of a piece of paper and the total of what you owe, or liabilities, on the other side. Then, by subtracting your liabilities from your assets you come up with the number which constitutes your financial net worth. Now it doesn't tell you what you're worth as a person, only what you're worth in monetary terms.

I said to Mr. Shoaff, "My financial statement isn't going to look too good." He said, "It's not important how good it looks. What *is* important is that you do it."

So I put together my first financial statement. I had lots of liabilities. I owed money to my parents, to the finance company, on my car, and to several other institutions who expected to be paid monthly. Now, on the asset side, I was scraping. I put down everything I could think of. I even included my shoes! After all, they were worth something. Wow, how embarrassing to have so little — after six years of working!

No doubt you're doing much better. But even if you're not, you need to have a financial statement. You don't have to post the results on a public bulletin board; it isn't important that you proclaim it to the community. But it's incredibly important that you know the score of your present financial game plan.

With your financial statement, start keeping good books of your income and expenses. Have you ever heard the expression, "I don't know where it all goes?" Never be the one to say it. From now on make a point of knowing exactly where it all goes and where it all comes from.

Hey, I found out that just making good money isn't enough. I found out that a person can make ten thousand dollars a month and still go broke. You say, "How can you go broke making ten thousand a month?" It's easy! Just spend eleven thousand.

And believe me, when you make ten thousand, it's not hard to spend eleven thousand. As someone once said, "If your outgo exceeds your income, your upkeep will become your downfall."

So become master over what you have and what you are. That's where the seeds of greatness are sown — great wealth, great health, great results, great influence, and great lifestyle. Take interest and even delight in doing the small things well. It will help you become a sophisticated person — one who knows the fundamental strategies for wealth and happiness.

There is a biblical saying that if you will be faithful to a few things, you will someday become the ruler over many things. That's it — that's the philosophy that counts. Life is reluctant to hand over fortune and responsibility to someone who messes up his or her paycheck. But assume responsibility for keeping score of your financial life and you have taken a major step to be trusted with a life of abundance.

★ THE WEALTH-AND-HAPPINESS ATTITUDE ★

I used to say, "I hate to pay my taxes."

Mr. Shoaff said, "Well, you can live that way if you want to — that's certainly one attitude."

I was a bit perplexed. I thought it was the only attitude to have. I wondered what he meant . . .

I used to say, "I hate to pay my bills."

And he said, "Well, you can live that way if you want to."

I thought it was the only way.

I used to say, "I hate to part with my money."

Mr. Shoaff said, "That's one choice for an attitude and lifestyle."

Finally, I asked, "Is there another way to feel about these things?"

Mr. Shoaff answered, "What if you said, 'I love to pay my taxes because I know that it is my part in the care and feeding of the goose that lays the golden eggs'? What if you said, 'I love to pay my bills, reduce my liabilities, and increase my assets'? What if you said, 'I love to part with my money and put it into circulation where it can help build a dynamic economy'? Wouldn't it be a better way if you learned to 'love to' rather than 'hate to'?"

What an incredible way to look at life! And although it took me a while to learn to say, truthfully, "I love to," the change in my life from hating to loving made a tremendous difference.

Mr. Shoaff even taught me to pay my car payments with enthusiasm. He said, "Next time you pay a hundred dollars on your installment loan, put a note inside the envelope that says, 'With great enthusiasm I send you this one hundred dollars.' " Smiling broadly, he continued, "You won't believe what a stir this will cause on the other end. They don't get many notes like that. But most important, you won't believe what will happen on your end. You'll feel in control, carrying with you a philosophy that brings joy instead of frustration."

Financial independence? You can achieve it. Why not start today? All it takes is the discipline to apply the 70/30 rule to your life. Young or old, it's never too late to get on the right track.

STRATEGY FIVE

Master Time

Chapter 8

How to Be an Enlightened Time Manager

A few years ago while on a lecture tour in South Africa, I stumbled across a short essay by Arnold Bennet on the subject of time. I liked it so much that I want to share it with you:

Time is the inexplicable raw material of everything. With it all is possible; without it, nothing. The supply of time is truly a daily miracle, an affair genuinely astonishing when one examines it.

You wake up in the morning, and lo! Your purse is magically filled with twenty-four hours of the unmanufactured tissue of the universe of your life. It is yours. It is the most precious of possessions . . . no one can take it from you. It is unstealable. And no one receives either more or less than you receive.

In the realm of time, there is no aristocracy of wealth and no aristocracy of intellect. Genius is never rewarded by even an extra hour a day. And there is no punishment. Waste your infinitely precious commodity as much as you will and the supply will never be withheld from you.

Moreover, you cannot draw on the future. Impossible to get into debt! You can only waste the passing moment. You cannot waste tomorrow; it is kept for you.

I have said the affair is a miracle, is it not? You have this twenty-four hours of daily time to live. Out of it you want to spin health, pleasure, money, contentment, respect, and the evolution of your immortal soul.

Its right use, its most effective use is a matter of the highest urgency and of the most thrilling actuality. All depends on that. Your happiness — the elusive prize that you are all clutching for, my friend — depends on that.

If one cannot arrange that an income of twenty-four hours shall exactly cover all proper items of expenditure, one does muddle one's whole life indefinitely.

We shall never have any more time. We have, and we have always had, all the time there is.

★ THE FOUR ATTITUDES TOWARD THE MANAGEMENT OF TIME ★

Time is the most precious commodity we have. Therefore, how we manage it has the most profound effect on how our lives turn out. Every one of us has developed an attitude about time, whether we are conscious of this or not. This attitude determines the approach a person takes toward his or her allotment of time.

There are four separate attitudes about time. Each creates a distinctly different lifestyle:

The Drifter Mentality

Drifters ignore the subject of time altogether. They choose to keep their lifestyle as unstructured as possible. They let their lives meander aimlessly, like tumbleweed in a light desert wind, enjoying the uncertainty and spontaneity that accompanies such a life.

If they hold a job it's usually a temporary one because they rebel against any structure, any attempt to harness time. The typical drifter will say, "I've been late all my life. I can't ever seem to get a handle on my time. The heck with it! I'll just take it easy and get where I'm going when I'm good and ready."

Anything wrong with this attitude? Who am I to say? It's *your* life. But if you find yourself attracted to this mode of living, consider that this attitude of drifting along the highways and byways of life will stand in the way of any chance for real progress. You can't *drift* your way to a better life.

The Nine-to-Five Time Manager

Another group of people, perhaps the majority, has adopted an attitude about time that falls somewhere between the drifter and the workaholic. These people seem to function best with a moderate level of stress. They can handle only so many projects at one time. They like to have their evenings free — to "smell the flowers" all through life.

A man works for a company, then decides to own his own business. But as his responsibilities mount, as he sees how he must come to work before anyone else and leave long after the janitor has left, he thinks, "I would rather work for someone else. Let *them* have all the glory *and* the headaches."

Is he wrong? Of course not — not if his only two options are either working around the clock or working in a nine-to-five job. (You'll soon see, when we discuss the fourth attitude about time, these are not his only options.) When he tried to run his own company, he exceeded the maximum level of time commitment he can handle comfortably. And so, he decides to walk away from the challenge, convinced that for him the price for success is too high.

Not everyone can handle the high price of success. Not only is this true in running an independent business, it's equally true of many corporate executives I know. Here's a story which illustrates that some people should put limits on the price they pay:

A little girl asks her mother, "Why doesn't Daddy play with me? He comes home from work, and right away he goes to his den. And as soon as dinner is over, he's off to do some more work. I want to play with my daddy. Doesn't he love me anymore?"

So Mom, fighting back tears of her own loneliness and pain, tries to explain, "Honey, your daddy is very busy. He loves you very much, and that is why he works so hard. He has so much work to do at his office that he has to bring some of it home."

The little girl thinks for a moment about what her mother just told her. Suddenly, her eyes brighten and she says, "Well, if he can't get all his work done at the office, why don't they just put him in a slower group?"

Why not, indeed! There's a limit a person should pay for financial and career success. And that limit comes when other important values are sacrificed at the altar of material success.

I know . . . I, too, went after some things in my life, only to find out later that I paid too much. Had I known how much they were going to cost before I began, I never would have paid the high price.

The Workaholic

The old-fashioned concept of success, as typified by Willy Loman in *Death of a Salesman*, is the kind which keeps a person working longer and harder. For the workaholic there is never enough work. He or she works ten, twelve, fourteen hours a day. The workaholic will take two jobs, working them back to back. Satisfaction only comes when sleep is fought off, enjoyment is denied, and more tasks are finished.

We all know the results of this kind of behavior. While often eliciting admiration from outsiders, the workaholic's behavior can result in the alienation of family, loss of health, and eventually a crisis of values.

Ironically, the workaholic is not always the one who makes the most money. That's because he or she is often more task-oriented than results-oriented.

If I had to choose between the three attitudes about time which I have so far described, I would be hard-pressed to choose the superior one. But fortunately there is one other attitude about time which I consider ideal:

The Enlightened Time Manager

The fourth and most enlightened approach to time borrows from the other three. The enlightened time manager allots time for every aspect of his life. He even allots time for drifting, by scheduling time to do nothing. Like the nine-to-five person, he knows to limit the hours of work and to have quality time for other important values, such as family. And like the workaholic, he would never be afraid to work long hours — but only when necessary.

What makes the enlightened time manager enlightened is his ability to schedule himself to work only so many hours and still get more done than the workaholic. How does he do that? Simply by working smarter, not always longer — by focusing on more productivity per hour instead of putting in more hours.

Enlightened time managers look for new ways to multiply their productivity. In other words, they develop wealth by the use of leverage.

Leverage allows you to multiply your resources many times over. For example, you can leverage money by borrowing wisely to purchase real estate or to build a business. You can leverage time by multiplying your efforts through the recruitment of an expanding sales force or by delegating less productive work to competent employees.

★ THE MASTERY OF TIME ★

Here's a key to understanding the management of time. Either you run your day or your day will run you. It's really a matter of deciding to be in charge. You see, it's much too easy to relinquish control, to hand over the reins of authority and lose the ability to direct time.

One of the best ways to start regaining control of our time is to learn the most effective time-management word. Do you know what it is? The word is "no." Learn to say "no."

I still have difficulty with this one. It's so easy to say yes to everything — to be a "nice" person. The result of saying yes is that we spend long hours trying to get ourselves out of obligations we never should have agreed to in the first place. It's one of the great time-wasters.

I finally learned to say no nicely. How? This is what I do. I say: "No, I don't think I can. But if that changes, I'll give you a call." Now isn't it better to call people with good news and let them know you can do it after all? Try it, it works! A friend of mine, Ron Reynolds, is fond of saying, "Don't let your mouth overload your back."

Another way to regain control of your day is this: When you work, work; and when you play, play. Mixing the two never works. All you end up doing is cheating yourself both ways. If you work and play at the same time, you'll miss the joy that comes from great accomplishment and the complete release that is the gift of pure play.

I know . . . I used to say, "I've got to get my family to the beach. I've promised them that we'll go. What will they think of me if I don't take them?" So I'd take them to the beach, all the while thinking, "I should be at the office. How come I'm at the beach? I have so much to do. How can I cut this trip short so I can get back to work?" The result? I would mess up a potentially wonderful time by thinking "work" during playtime.

I also used to do the opposite. I'd say, "I'm going to take off at three to ride my motorcycle on the back roads." Guess what I'd be thinking about for the rest of the day? That's right, riding on the back roads.

Now when I go on a lecture tour to Spain, Africa, or Australia, I make it a work trip. Every day is filled with lectures, interviews, and conferences. But once my business obligations are over, I take time to play, to explore, to enjoy. It's been a valuable lesson.

A friend of mine, a successful builder, has created a schedule of working a week and taking off a week. He calls it his work-a-week-play-a-week plan. In reality, when you count the weekends, he really plays for nine days and works for five days. Quite a luxury, right? However, let me tell you this: During those five days, he works; he *really* works. You can't believe the whirlwind of activities he creates. The dust really flies as secretaries, accountants, architects, and superintendents meet with him hour upon hour. His five days are made up of maximum effort. He goes all out, nonstop. Then he shuts everything off and leaves to play with his family. Amazing!

Self-Knowledge

One of the great rules of creative time management is this: KNOW THYSELF. Each of us has a unique biological clock which daily controls the peaks and ebbs of our productivity.

Find out when you are at your most energetic. If you are most productive early in the morning, take advantage of this by scheduling your biggest projects as the first order of the day. For example, if your career involves persuading people, arrange to schedule appointments over breakfast.

But if the opposite is true for you and you have a hard time remembering your name until lunch time, schedule your most demanding business activities for the afternoon and evening.

Next, analyze your habits. For example, if you're not good at keeping your paperwork up to date or if you've promised yourself for years to keep better records and balance the checkbook and you still haven't done it — accept it, and get someone to help you. You're not likely to change.

Your weaknesses don't have to harm you if you learn to delegate responsibilities. This, too, is part of creative time management.

A few years ago my staff came to the conclusion that I am a poor courier. Because I travel constantly, they would often ask me to deliver documents to people in the city to which I was going. "Sure, no problem," I'd reply as I absentmindedly put the papers in my coat pocket. I recall several times hearing about these undelivered documents from my dry cleaners . . .

After awhile, my staff approached me as if I were a five-year-old. On one occasion they said, "This document has to go to New York. Will you be *sure* to deliver it *this* time?" I said, "Of course. You can count on me. Hey, I'm not flaky." Needless to say, the document was still in my briefcase when I returned.

So now the word is out. Every new employee is indoctrinated by my staff: "Don't give the chairman anything to deliver. He's good at a lot of things, but he's a poor courier. Make other arrangements."

And that's my point. There is nothing shameful about admitting that you aren't good at everything — as long as you are wise enough not to let your weaknesses stop you from accomplishing your goals. Indeed, knowing oneself is a crucial aspect of time management.

The Telephone

We have all learned to take the telephone for granted. It's so common today that instead of having one in every home, we now have a phone in every room and, soon, there will be one in every car. And yet, few of us have taken the time to analyze how to use the telephone for maximum effectiveness. Thus, we need to recognize that while it has incredible potential for efficiency, the telephone also can be one of the most disruptive time-wasters in our lives.

You see, just as the telephone is a remarkable tool for you, it is also a remarkable tool for everyone else. Just as you have the ability to reach others in seconds, so do others have the ability to reach you instantly. This reality can play havoc with any daily plan or routine.

Therefore, make sure the telephone is there primarily for *your* convenience. Gain control over who can reach you and when. If you have the luxury of having a secretary, train him or her to screen your phone calls effectively. Or use an answering machine so that you can return phone calls at *your* convenience.

Remember, also, that the telephone allows others to control your time, even at home. That means that unless you're careful, others can also intrude on your family and leisure time. Don't let that happen. During social times with friends or family, find a way to avoid answering the telephone. You can use an answering service, an answering machine, or you can simply pull out the plug. Your family and friends are too important to have the ever-insistent ringing of the telephone monopolize the time you've reserved for them.

In addition to controlling your incoming phone calls, there

is a simple way to better manage your outgoing calls: Have an agenda. All of us waste time and money on inefficient phone conversations. Have you ever heard yourself saying, "Let's see, there was something else I wanted to talk with you about. I just can't think of it right now. I'll have to call you back"? We've all said that at one time or another. It's a great time-waster, and it also appears unprofessional.

Solution? Before every phone call write down the key points you want to cover. It will make each conversation more effective, shorter, and more professional. It will also give you a record of each call.

Should you have to recall a telephone conversation, you'll have the information in front of you. For example, you can say, "John, how are you doing on those four things we talked about the other day?" And should John reply, "What four things? We didn't talk about *that*," you can calmly show John your written record of your conversation.

Time-Effective Organization

We all do things as a result of long-standing habits. This becomes a wasteful luxury, however, when we want to be more efficient. So take the time to analyze your work procedures. Is your filing method up-to-date? What about your bookkeeping? Today there are many efficient ways to increase productivity through electronic means. Our age has brought with it tremendous possibilities for processing more information faster. You might want to take advantage of some of them.

In my office I have a computer that can do the most amazing things and save a great deal of time. In addition, I also have a portable machine that I can use when traveling. After entering the information, I merely transfer it via a modem to my main computer. What a time saver!

Of course, these new electronic marvels can cause time loss as well. Millions have purchased computers in order to balance their checkbooks or keep telephone numbers. That's like getting into a car and driving over to visit your next-door neighbors. So *do* analyze carefully how to use these new electronic tools. And if your business is more sophisticated, have an expert help you. Remember, you don't need to be good at everything if you have others cover your weaknesses.

Asking the Right Questions

When managing people, one of the greatest time-savers is asking questions — more specifically, asking the *right* questions. In behavioral psychology we learn that everything is a result of something else. And when a problem arises, it is usually a clue that a deeper problem lies beneath the surface.

The best way to get to the bottom of things is to not jump to conclusions but to ask questions . . .

If Mary isn't making sales we could say, "Okay, we need to give Mary a lecture about making sales." Or maybe we should ask her supervisor, "Why isn't Mary making sales?" The supervisor might say, "She isn't making enough calls." So we dig further. "Why isn't she making enough calls?" And we are told, "It's because she doesn't start her day early enough." I suppose we could stop here and try to motivate Mary to start earlier. But, instead, we ask one more question, "Why isn't Mary starting her day earlier?" *Now*, we've finally gotten to the heart of the issue. Perhaps Mary is having a personal problem. Perhaps it's not her sales skills that need improvement.

The real causes to important problems are usually buried several layers deep. By becoming good at asking the right questions you can save yourself enormous time by getting to the root of problems a lot faster.

★ FOUR WAYS OF THINKING ON PAPER ★

One of the greatest tools for successful time management is having the ability to think on paper. Building a successful enterprise is like building a house. You visualize the ideas, put them on paper, and execute them. In my company we have a saying: OPERATE FROM DOCUMENT NOT FROM THOUGHT.

Building a day also requires thinking on paper. It's just about over when a person wakes up in the morning and says, "Let's see, what shall I do today?" It's *too late*. About the best thing that person can do is take the rest of the day off and start planing the next day, the next week, the next month.

Thinking on paper is a creative process. There is much more to it than just making a "to do" list. In fact, there are four different but essential methods that you should use to plan your life:

Your Journal

In my lectures and intensive seminars I spend a great deal of time promoting the use of journals. I do so because it's my conviction that they are invaluable tools for the serious students of successful living.

A journal is a gathering place for all the good information and wisdom that comes your way. Good ideas can originate from almost anywhere. Perhaps you may hear a particularly meaningful sermon. Or you may read a bit of information you can use. You might even think of a great idea while driving.

The point is: DON'T LET GOOD IDEAS ESCAPE YOU. A great idea can change your life — if you capture it. Have a journal with you at all times, no matter where you are.

A Project Book

As ambitious and busy as you are, you have many projects on which you're working and people with whom you're dealing. Busy people like you often feel as if they're jugglers who must keep all the plates spinning at the same time. It's not easy.

One of the best ways to stay in control is to get a project book — a ring binder with tabs in it. If you're working with people, allot a separate section in your binder to each individual. Under each person's tab, keep all pertinent information about him or her. Note each person's performance, family history, goals, strengths, needs, or anything else you consider relevant. As a manager, you may also want to have information such as sales records or performance charts. This way, should you need to evaluate performance, you have concrete, usable information.

Now, depending on your particular business or profession, you may also want to "tab" each office or department. Or you may want to categorize items project by project — that's up to you. The key is to *centralize* all data so that you can focus on it without having to spend wasted hours hunting for information in countless forgotten files.

This concept of having a project book will also work for your personal affairs . . .

For example, you can "keep tabs" on each one of your children. Does keeping information about your children sound a bit cold? Then let me ask you: Do you remember your child's latest report card? If so, how does it compare to the one before? What event did your child ask you to attend? Do you have it written down? Remember the last meaningful one-to-one conversation the two of you had? What was your child's main concern?

You see, children remember all interactions with their parents. Unfortunately, we as parents are often preoccupied and inattentive. Keeping a separate section on each child can always remind us of the essentials.

Naturally, your personal financial affairs will also benefit from this system by allowing you to refer at a glance to all your investments, insurance policies, and the like.

Now, do you really *need* a journal or a project book to get by? Of course not! If all you want is to get by, none of this really matters. But for those of you on the journey to wealth and happiness, these techniques can accelerate your progress beyond belief.

A Calendar

Another method of organizing your thoughts on paper is by using a daily calendar. Now when I talk about a calendar I don't mean the kind that barely gives you enough space to write in your appointments. The kind I mean is called a "Day-Timer." (Day-Timers is also the name of the company.) The Day-Timer is a daily log of your appointments and schedules. But it's a lot more. It has a place to keep track of business expenses, meeting results, phone conversations, and "to do" lists.

Your Day-Timer can also be used as a gathering place for those daily or weekly highlights you wish to log into your journal or project book. Think of it as the central location from which you process all your information of the day, the week, the month, and even the year.

A Game Plan

A game plan can make all the difference in the world with respect to how your game of life turns out. The term "game plan" is ironic because, even though we seem to understand the importance of mapping out a strategy for a football or basketball game, few of us take the time to make a game plan for our lives.

Here's the first and most important rule for your life's game plan: DON'T START YOUR DAY UNTIL YOU HAVE IT FINISHED. Because each day is a priceless mosaic in your lifetime strategy for wealth and happiness, always plan your day before you start. And do it every day. Yes, I know, all this writing can be tedious. But remember, value is the fruitful result of effort, not of hope.

Once you have mastered the art of planning your day, every day, you are ready to graduate to the next level of higher success. The next key is: DON'T START THE WEEK UNTIL YOU HAVE IT FINISHED.

Plan your week before you start it. Imagine what your life will be like if you ask yourself on Sunday night, "What do I want to accomplish this week?" Yes, I know, it's a bit of a stretch, but if you learn to plan your days as part of your *overall* game plan for the week, all the parts will fit much better. As a result, each day will be that much more effective.

Once you master your planning for a week, you are able to plan your life one month at a time. Therefore, the next key is: DON'T START YOUR MONTH UNTIL IT'S FINISHED.

By following this rule, your weeks and days become part of a bigger design. You are developing a long-term view of your life, gaining greater perspective, because you are now planning.

And you'll be learning to coordinate your daily, weekly, and monthly goals with your three-month, six-month, and one-year goals.

Hey, it's going to take great discipline on your part. But when you accomplish this, you will be called a master. It may be a "high road" to the mastery of time, but I'm sure you'll enjoy the view, the taste, and the company of other masters like you!

★ HOW TO PREPARE A GAME PLAN ★

There are two things you should understand about creating game plans. First, a game plan acts like a spread sheet, but instead of listing numbers, it lists activities. Second, you can use the game-plan technique for either a single project or a variety of concurrent projects.

Here's how it works: On a sheet of graph paper make vertical columns of the number of days this plan is to cover. Then, on the left side of the paper make a heading called "activities." Under this heading list all the activities to be performed within that time frame.

For example, let's say you're working on launching a campaign for a new product. For each activity required (sales conferences, advertising support, packaging, market research), determine the deadline that must be met and plot it on the spread sheet. Then calculate the days it will take to accomplish the task and block them on your game-plan sheet. The final result is a clear visual presentation of the tasks before you.

Game plans are frustrating to create. You may tear up several before producing the perfect one. But they are frustrating only because you're finding it difficult to prioritize all your projects. However, once you put your game plan together you will enjoy an enormously satisfying feeling.

Keep your game plan where you can see it. Display it on your office wall or in your project book. It will serve as a constant reminder of the tasks at hand.

Game plans are both exciting and painful. They are painful because they keep reminding you to get on with your plans. They are also painful when you fall behind schedule. But they are exciting, too, because you see the magic of dreams and plans turning into reality. This is *immensely* rewarding. The feeling you get is not unlike that of a great artist surveying a completed canvas. It's the incredible feeling of being in charge.

A well-fashioned day, with a beginning and an end, a purpose and a content, a color and a character, a feel and a texture — this well-fashioned day takes its place among the many and becomes a valuable memory and treasure. And as one well-fashioned day turns into another, a life emerges that is a masterpiece, an equity of experience and spirit. For as someone once said, "At midnight the winged messengers come and gather up all these pieces and take them off to wherever the mosaic is kept. And surely, on occasion, one messenger says to another, "Wait 'til you see *this* one."

STRATEGY SIX

Surround

Yourself

with

Winners

Chapter 9

The Principle of Association

One of the major influences shaping the person you want to be is also one of the least understood. It is your association with others — the people you allow into your life. Have you ever thought about how others shape your life? The thought didn't even occur to me until Mr. Shoaff said, "Jim, never underestimate the power of influence."

Of course he was right. The influence of those around us is so powerful, so subtle, so gradual that often we don't even realize how it can affect us.

Think about it. If you're around people who spend all their income, chances are excellent that you will become a spendthrift. If you're around people who go to more wrestling games than concerts, you're likely to join in with them. Such is the power of peer pressure.

But it goes even further. If you're around people who think it's all right to cheat a little, you, too, might be persuaded to cut a few corners. People can really nudge you off course until one day, ten years down the road, you wake up asking yourself, "How did I get here anyway?"

And that's not a very happy moment . . .

To avoid wasting time with the wrong crowd you need to ask yourself three fundamental questions:

1. With whom do I spend time?

2. What are they doing to me?

3. Is this association okay with me?

Don't dismiss these questions. Take a look at the time you spend with each of your major associates. Is it positive and constructive or is it negative and destructive?

Not sure? Then think about these things:

- What have they got you doing?
- What have they got you listening to?
- What have they got you reading?
- Where have they got you going?
- What have they got you thinking?
- How have they got you talking?
- How have they got you feeling?
- What have they got you saying?

Finally, after you have really pondered these, ask yourself this one final question: Are my present associations helping me grow in the direction I have chosen through goal-setting? If you are fortunate enough to answer yes to this question, I'm happy for you. But if you are not so sure, then it's time to evaluate your relationships with some of the key players in your life.

It's so easy to dismiss this question of influence. The "guy" says, "I live here, but it doesn't matter. I'm around these people, but they don't bother me." Well, he's wrong. Everything matters! This is a good phrase to remember: EVERYTHING MATTERS.

This book is different from many others because it deals with reality, not wishful thinking. In fact, one of the main purposes of this book is to get you to say: "The days of kidding myself are over. I really want to know what I have become and what I am becoming. I want to know what my strengths and weaknesses are, what has power over me, what's influencing me, what I've allowed to affect my life."

So take a look and then another. Everything worthwhile deserves a second look, especially the power of influence.

Perhaps you've heard the story about the little swallow . . .

It was covering one eye with its wing and crying bitterly. An owl flew by and asked, "Little bird, what's wrong?" The swallow pulled away its wing and showed a gash where once it had an eye. "Now I understand," hooted the owl, blinking, "You're crying because the crow pecked out your eye!" "No," replied the bird sadly, "I'm not crying because the crow pecked out my eye; I'm crying because I *let* him."

Is there someone who is pecking away at your vision? Is there anyone who tries to blind you from seeing your dreams? Hey, it's easy to let influences shape our lives, especially negative influences. It's easy to let associations determine our direction, to let persuasion overwhelm us, to let tides overtake us, and to let pressures mold us. The question is, is this what you want?

Are you becoming, achieving, and acquiring what you want, or are you letting others steal your dreams?

★ DISASSOCIATION ★

If after analyzing your present relationships you determine that you have some weeds in your garden of association, there are a couple of things you can do.

First, you can separate yourself from those people who are destructive to your well-being. I admit this is a tough thing to do, especially if its a family member. But if you have someone who finds a great deal of pleasure in trying to peck away at your dreams, goals, or beliefs, get rid of his or her influence.

Remember, it could be the choice that saves the quality of your life.

Of course life is rarely that simple. Sometimes we find ourselves having to spend time with unpleasant people — co-workers, business associates, and others. In those circumstances where you cannot fully disassociate yourself, try *limited* association.

There are also those situations where superficially pleasant associations can have a long-term negative effect on our lives. If you spend two nights a week drinking with your buddies, your life may eventually spin dangerously out of balance. The consequences five, ten, twenty years from now can be devastating.

It's easy to remain mediocre. All you need to do is spend major time on minor things with minor people. Sophisticated people weigh their actions. They know what a major is and what a minor is. They don't often get confused by such things.

Of course, sophisticated people do have casual friends. The difference is that instead of spending a great deal of time with them, they spend relaxed, relatively unimportant time with them. They just don't *squander* their time on minor friendships and "good-time Charleys."

It's your life. You can spend your time with whomever you want and however you want. But I don't think you invested in this book for me to humor you. You must take a look at your priorities and values, including your associations, and evaluate them. Your time on this earth is too short to spend it less than wisely.

★ EXPANDED ASSOCIATION ★

From disassociation let's move to a happier topic: expanded association. Here's the law of expanded association: SPEND

MORE TIME WITH THE RIGHT PEOPLE. Who are those *right* people? That depends on your goals and objectives. But generally look for people of substance and culture — people who spend time reflecting on the meaning of life and who accomplish great things through discipline and perseverance.

That's what Mr. Shoaff advised me shortly after we met. He said, "If you truly want success, you've got to get around the right people." And then, with a wry look he added, "Of course, in your present circumstances you'll have to plot and scheme to do that." And that was true! I *did* have to plot and scheme to get around the right people.

During those early days, when called upon to give a sales presentation, I would frequently park my disintegrating jalopy-minus-muffler several blocks away. Invariably someone would ask me, "By the way, Jim, how did you get here?" — to which I would respond, "Oh, someone dropped me off." Of course, that someone was *me* dropping myself off in my noisy "bomb."

It's really not all that difficult to associate with successful people. Just get involved in your community. I have a friend who started a sales business. She then joined her town's chamber of commerce, became active on a few committees, and before she knew it found herself invited to play tennis with some of the city's more influential people. You see, it's not so hard to create new associations.

Also, as we discussed in an earlier chapter, make an investment in a rich person's appetite. Take a rich person out for a meal. There's no telling what you can learn in an hour or two of wealth-oriented talk.

In expanding your associations, take a look at your life's priorities. It's called associating with a purpose.

For example, find some successful people to help you with your success plan; find some healthy people to encourage you to have an exercise and nutrition plan; find someone who knows how to live to teach you the secrets of a rewarding lifestyle. And don't be embarrassed about cultivating the friendships of these people. Most successful people love to share their knowledge with others. (It's probably why they're successful in the first place.)

Successful people seek out those they admire. They understand that inspiration and knowledge can be gained from the right type of association. I am no exception to this rule. I have such an association, a person with whom I like to spend as much time as possible. He's a big-game hunter, a millionaire, a traveler, and an entrepreneur. He's also one of the world's great philosophers.

My friend has many skills, but two are positively uncanny . . .

First, he has the ability to absorb a day's events in minute detail. Not only does he remember each day, I believe he can also remember every day of his adult life. He is able to recall every book he's ever read. He seems to retain every fact he learns. If I had a choice of going to a foreign country myself or having him visit and recount his trip to me, I would almost choose the latter. Why? Because he doesn't miss anything that's important. He absorbs every event like a sponge.

His second talent is his expressiveness. When he returns from a trip, he describes in vivid detail the sounds and colors of the country, the customs and concerns of its people, the minor experiences and the major happenings of his journey. He can put all that he saw, touched, and felt into exciting, vibrant words.

As he recounts a trip his listeners can feel the crash of the waterfall, the cool breeze of the northern winds, the colors and smells of the cities and the countryside. What a gift he gives those of us privileged to know him!

What value can one put on such a unique association? I don't know, but I can say with confidence that from our association I've expanded my knowledge, my perception, my skill, my enterprise, and my lifestyle many times over.

Where do *you* go for your intellectual feast? Pity the person who has a favorite restaurant but not a favorite thinker. That person has taken care to feed his body but not his mind and soul.

Today, thanks to Gutenberg, Marconi, and other pioneers in the field of recording information, we can also associate across the seas and throughout the centuries. Perhaps you can't meet the person, but you can read his words or listen to his recorded voice. Churchill, Aristotle, and Lincoln are no longer alive, but their words can still awe, inspire, and instruct.

Association — it's one of the seven strategies for wealth and happiness. Keep the weeds of negative influence from your life. Instead, "farm" the seeds of constructive influence. You will not believe the harvest of good fortune you will reap!

STRATEGY SEVEN

Learn the Art

of

Living Well

Chapter 10

Your Road to a Richer Lifestyle

In his role as teacher, Mr. Shoaff would continually challenge me. As soon as I'd apply his principles in one area, he would immediately bring up another principle of fundamental importance.

Once I began to make my way in the marketplace and make more money, he said, "Jim, don't just learn how to earn, learn how to live!"

I didn't understand. In fact, I wasn't even paying that much attention. "Here I am," I thought, "working hard, striving to reach goals, seeing success. What is he talking about? What does he think I'm missing? *What else is there?*"

Reading my thoughts, Mr. Shoaff smiled and said, "Jim, there are some people who have beautiful things surrounding them, and yet they feel little happiness; others have hoarded huge sums of money and yet are poor in spirit and find little joy in their lives. I want you to learn the art of designing a lifestyle, the art of learning how to live."

"Well," I replied, "I can think about this when I actually have lots of money. Right now I should just learn to make it, don't you think?"

"No, Jim," he said, shaking his head, "it's easier to learn the art of designing a lifestyle with small amounts. In fact, it starts with two quarters."

"Two quarters?" I exclaimed. "How can anyone possibly develop a lifestyle with two quarters?"

Mr. Shoaff chuckled. The consummate salesman, he knew he finally had my full attention. "Imagine that you are getting your shoes shined. Your shoeshine boy is doing an incredible job for you. In fact, you're getting one of the world's all-time great shines. As you pay him for the shine, you consider what kind of tip to give him. You think, 'Shall I give him a quarter or two quarters?' If two different amounts come to mind, always go for the higher amount; become a two-quarter person."

"I must be missing something," I thought. Perplexed, I asked, "What difference does it make — one quarter or two quarters?"

"It makes all the difference in the world. If you said, 'Well, I'll just give him one quarter,' that would affect you for the rest of the day. You'll start feeling a little guilty, just a *bit* insecure. And sometime during your day you'd look at the sheen on your leather and say, 'I certainly am cheap. One lousy quarter tip for a shine like this!'"

"On the other hand," he added, "if you go for the two quarters you'll feel prosperous and confident all day long. You can't believe the difference that a two-quarter mentality can make."

Years later a man in Detroit came up after one of my seminars and said, "Mr. Rohn, you inspired me tonight with your description of the two-quarters attitude. I've decided to change my whole life. You'll hear from me someday." And he left.

Sure enough, a few months later, when I was again lecturing in Detroit, the same man walked up to the podium with a big grin on his face and said, "Do you remember me?"

"Of course I do," I answered. "You're the man who said he was going to change his life."

He nodded his head and said, "I've got to tell you a story."

"After your last seminar I started to think about ways to

begin changing my life, and I decided to start with my family. I have two lovely teenage daughters — the best kids anyone could ask for. They never give me any trouble. However, I've always given them a hard time. One of the things they dearly love to do is attend rock concerts to see their favorite performers. Now I've always given them a hard time with this. They would ask for permission to go and I would say, 'No, I don't want you to go. The music is too loud. You'll ruin your hearing. And besides, it's the wrong crowd.'

"Then the same thing would always happen. They would beg, 'Please, Daddy, we want to go. We don't give you any trouble. We're good girls. Please let us go.'

"After they'd beg long enough I would reluctantly throw the money at them and say, 'Okay, if you have to have it *that* bad . . .'

"That's when I decided to start making some changes in my life. Here's what I did: I saw this announcement for a concert with one of my daughters' favorite performers, so I went to the ticket office and bought the tickets myself.

"When I got home I handed them the envelope and said, 'Here are tickets to the upcoming rock concert. I know the group is one of your favorites.'

"Jim," the man continued, tears welling up in his eyes, "you should have seen the look on their faces. I told them the begging days are over. What a hug I got! Then I made them promise me not to open the envelope until they got to the concert.

"And you know what! Because I got them tickets for the tenth row center, I had so much fun all evening just imagining their excitement.

"My real reward came when they arrived home. One of them landed on my lap and the other wrapped her arms around my neck, and they both said, 'Daddy, you're the greatest.'"

What a wonderful story! And what a compelling example of how it's possible, with just a small change in attitude, to transform one's lifestyle. It's just a matter of learning to be generous of spirit and learning to develop a two-quarter mentality in a one-quarter-thinking world.

★ SAME MONEY, DIFFERENT STYLE ★

Here's an important thought: BE HAPPY WITH WHAT YOU HAVE WHILE PURSUING WHAT YOU WANT.

I try to live this one every day of my life.

It's really not so hard to learn the art of living. Even people with modest means can experience a sophisticated lifestyle. They simply save up some of their soda money for a bottle of fine wine. Or they skip going to the movies and attend the theater. Or by saving up their money all year they have enough for a trip to Europe or a fine work of art.

Don't spend all your money a quarter at a time. Save up and buy something special — something fine, of lasting value, or something which will give you rich memories for a lifetime. Remember, all that candy money can add up to a small fortune. And for a sophisticated person, quality is far more important than quantity. Better a few treasures than a house full of junk.

Lifestyle, as I define it here, is a matter of awareness, values, education, and disciplined taste. It is an art that brings joy as it's practiced. It's the deliberate decision to savor and enjoy all the experiences and possibilities of life.

Lifestyle means expanding your knowledge and experiences from the influence of books, people, films, and new adventures. So take care to enjoy and learn from everything and everyone with whom you come in contact.

Think of something you can do today to make you feel richer and better about yourself and your life; make a phone call to reserve tickets for a concert, buy some recordings of fine music, send flowers, send a thank-you note, plan a trip, begin to read a classic.

Still can't think of anything to do? I'll bet within fifty miles of where you are right now there are some places you have never seen, some foods you've never tasted, some experiences you've never had.

It's true for me. As you know, I grew up in Idaho, where a part of the great Yellowstone National Park lies. And yet I've never been to Yellowstone. Imagine that! Millions have traveled from around the world to see the grizzlies and Old Faithful, and I, a native of Idaho, have never been there. I've been to Africa, but not to Yellowstone.

Do you have a "Yellowstone" story in your life? Are you a New Yorker who's never been to the Statue of Liberty? Or a Texan who's never been to the Alamo? Or a Canadian who's never visited Ottawa? Then, like me, you are missing some wonderful opportunities to experience an expanded lifestyle.

Let's all set new goals to not miss anything, especially those things that are within our reach. It might take a little initiative on our parts, but think what rewards await us! All we need to do is allow a conscious act to well up from a unique thought. And this act will bridge our dreams with the reality of new experience.

By now you know I have a healthy respect for the value of material wealth in life. But money can also be overrated, even worshipped. It is often given powers that it simply does not possess.

I remember saying to Mr. Shoaff, "If I had more money I'd be happy." But he replied, "The key to happiness is not more. Happiness is an art to be studied and practiced. More money will only make you more of what you already are. *More* will only send you more quickly to your destination. So if you're inclined to be unhappy, you'll be luxuriously miserable with more money. If you're inclined to be nasty, wealth will make you a terror. And if you're inclined to drink a little too much, more money will only enable you to waste yourself in booze.

"On the other hand, if you master the art of lifestyle and happiness, more money will help you to amplify your happiness and inner wealth."

Lifestyle is style over amount. And style is an art — the art of living. You can't buy style with money. You can't buy good taste with money. You can only buy *more* with money.

Lifestyle is culture — the appreciation of good music, dance, art, sculpture, literature, and plays. It's a taste for the fine, the unique, the beautiful.

Mortimer Adler, the philosopher, said, "If we don't go for the higher tastes, we will settle for the lower ones."

So remember the quest. It's to have the best in the time available to us. It's not the amount, it's the value.

Lifestyle also means rewarding excellence wherever you find it by not taking the small things of life for granted. Let me illustrate this with a personal anecdote:

My lady friend and I were on a trip to Carmel, California, for some shopping and exploring. On the way we stopped at a service station. As soon as we parked our car in front of the pumps, a young man, about eighteen or nineteen, came bouncing out to the car and with a big smile said, "Can I help you?"

"Yes," I answered. "A full tank of gas, please."

I wasn't prepared for what followed. In this day and age of self-service and deteriorating customer treatment, this young man checked every tire, washed every window — even the sunroof — singing and whistling the whole time. We couldn't believe both the quality of service and his upbeat attitude about his work.

When he brought the bill I said to the young man, "Hey, you really have taken good care of us. I appreciate it."

He replied, "I really enjoy working. It's fun for me and I

get to meet nice people like you."

This kid was really something!

I said, "We're on our way to Carmel and we want to get some milkshakes. Can you tell us where we can find the nearest Baskin-Robbins?"

"Baskin-Robbins is just a few blocks away," he said as he gave us exact directions. Then he added, "Don't park out front — park around to the side so your car won't get sideswiped."

What a kid!

As we got to the ice cream store we ordered milkshakes, except that instead of two, we ordered three. Then we drove back to the station. Our young friend dashed out to greet us. "Hey, I see you got your milkshakes."

"Yes, and this one is for you!"

His mouth fell open. "For me?"

"Sure. With all the fantastic service you gave us, I couldn't leave you out of the milkshake deal."

"Wow!" was his astonished reply.

As we drove off I could see him in my rear-view mirror just standing there, grinning from ear to ear.

Now, what did this little act of generosity cost me? Only about two dollars. (This number has a way of cropping up, doesn't it?) You see, it's not the money, it's the style.

I must have been feeling especially creative that day. On our arrival in Carmel I drove directly to a flower shop. As we walked inside I said to the florist, "I need a long-stemmed rose for my lady to carry while we go shopping in Carmel."

The florist, a rather unromantic type, replied, "We sell them by the dozen."

"I don't need a dozen," I said, "just one."

"Well," he replied haughtily, "it will cost you two dollars."

"Wonderful," I exclaimed. "There's nothing worse than a cheap rose."

Selecting the rose with some deliberation, I handed it to my friend. She was so impressed! And the cost? *Two dollars.* Just two dollars. (A bit later she looked up and said, "Jim, I must be the only woman in Carmel today carrying a rose.")

Besides the two-quarter lesson, Mr. Shoaff taught me another lesson about tipping. He explained to me that the term "tip" comes from the words "to insure promptness."

"Now," he said, "if a tip is meant to insure promptness, when should one tip?"

I knew what he was driving at, but I was still thinking "average." "When you have a meal and the service is good, you leave a tip. If you get lousy service, no tip," was my reply.

"No, Jim, you don't understand. Sophisticated people don't take a chance on good service. They *insure* good service by giving the money up front."

Try it. The next time you have a special meal at a restaurant, ask the waiter or waitress to come to your table, put your arm on his or her shoulder, and say, "Here's five dollars. Would you take good care of me and my friend?"

As Mr. Shoaff said, "You won't believe what will happen. They will hover over your table. You won't have to wonder where they went or wait for a second cup of coffee."

Are you getting the message? Same money, different style.

★ LOVE AND FRIENDSHIP ★

Living life in style also means living a life of balance. And one of the most important ingredients of a balanced life is having someone to love and love you. If you have someone you care about there is nothing more valuable. One person caring about another represents life at its most abundant.

Protect love with a vengeance. Don't let anything stand in its way. If a chair gets in the way, I suggest you destroy the chair. Don't let anything block love.

It was wisely said long ago, "There are many treasures, but the greatest of these is love." In other words, it's better to live in a tent on the beach and know love than to live in a mansion all alone. Ask me . . . I know. Your family and your love must be cultivated like a garden. Time, effort, and imagination must be summoned constantly to keep it flourishing and growing.

Next to love, friendship is most important. It's priceless. Friends are those wonderful people who know all about you and still like you. Friends are those people who come in when everyone else is leaving. And because life offers no guarantees, be sure, on the way up, to make the kinds of friends who will take you in on the way down. Life has both ups and downs, and friends, true friends, will make the ups more exhilarating and the downs less devastating.

I do have one such friend. If I were unjustly thrown into a jail in some foreign country, it's him I would call. Do you know why I would call him? That's right, because he'd come. Now that's a friend — someone who would get you out of some foreign jail. And I know that if it would cost a fortune to get me out, he'd spend it. And if it took a long time, he'd take as long as it would take. That's a true friend. I hope you have a friend like this.

I also have some casual friends, acquaintances who would probably say, "Call me when you get back to the States." I guess we all have friends like that. The problem comes when we confuse their function in our lives with true friendship.

In conclusion, remember this: The good life is not an amount; it's an attitude, an act, an idea, a discovery, a search. The good life comes from a lifestyle that is fully developed, regardless of the size of your bank account; a lifestyle that provides you with a constant sense of joy in living; a lifestyle that fuels your desire to become a person of deep value and achievement. After all, what is wealth without character, industry without art, quantity without quality, enterprise without satisfaction, and possessions without joy?

You can become a person of culture who adds to the whole culture. You can be that person of unusual substance who possesses the style and individuality of which our children and their children can become the beneficiaries.

Chapter 11

The Day That Turns Your Life Around

We have come a long way together. In this book, I have shared a feast of ideas with you — strategies that are sure to satisfy your appetite for wealth and happiness. And yet, I must also share with you a concern.

You see, if you assimilate all the information in this book, you could probably call yourself an expert on the principles of wealth and happiness. Why, you could no doubt even give a lecture on the philosophical aspects of success and sound pretty impressive at that.

But you must do more in life than know the theory of how things are *supposed* to work. In the free enterprise system you must *act* to make things happen. Only *applied knowledge* counts.

So how do you go about bridging the gap between knowledge and action? Is there a third component that acts as a catalyst? Fortunately, there is. It is our emotions.

★ EMOTIONS ★

Emotions are the most powerful forces inside us. Under the power of emotions human beings can perform the most heroic (as well as the most barbaric) acts. To a great degree civilization itself can be defined as the intelligent channeling of human emotion. Emotions are the fuel and the mind is the pilot which together propel the ship of civilized progress.

Which emotions cause people to act? There are four basic ones; each or a combination of several can trigger the most incredible activity. The day that you allow these emotions to fuel your desire is the day you'll turn your life around.

Disgust

One usually does not equate the word "disgust" with positive action. And yet properly channeled, disgust can change a person's life.

The person who feels disgust has reached a point of no return. He or she is ready to throw down the gauntlet at life itself and say, "*I've had it!*"

That's what I said after my humiliating experience with the Girl Scout and her two-dollar cookies. "I've had it!" I said. "I don't want to live like this *a-ny-more*. I've had it with being broke. I've had it with being embarrassed, and I've had it with lying."

Yes, productive feelings of disgust come when a person says, "Enough is enough." Period.

The "guy" has finally had it with being a loser. He's had it with mediocrity. He's had it with those awful sick feelings of fear, pain, and humiliation. He sees his wife walking once more through the canned-goods aisle of the supermarket to buy a can of beans, and he knows what's going to happen. He knows she will look at the brand that costs sixty-nine cents and the brand that costs sixty-seven cents. And he knows that although she prefers the sixty-nine-cent brand, she will buy the one for sixty-seven cents. And he knows, all too well, the *reason* she will buy the cheaper can — to save two cents. *Two cents*! Our "guy," sick inside, says: "I've had it with being on my knees in the dust looking for pennies. We are not living like this *a-ny-more*."

Look out! This could be the day that turns a life around. Call it what you will — the "I've had it" day, the "never again" day, the "enough's enough" day. Whatever you call it, you can call it powerful! There is nothing so life-changing as gut-wrenching disgust.

Conversely, there is nothing more pitiful than mild disgust. Someone says, "I kind of think I've had it . . ." How pathetic, how spineless. There isn't enough fuel in that kind of emotion to propel a toy boat in a bathtub!

Decision

Most of us need to be pushed to the wall to make decisions. And once we reach that point, we have to deal with the conflicting emotions that come with making them. We have reached a fork in the road.

Now this fork can be a two-prong, three-prong, or even four-prong fork. No wonder that decision-making can create knots in our stomachs, keep us awake in the middle of the night, or make us break out in a cold sweat.

Making life-changing decisions can be likened to internal civil war. Conflicting armies of emotions, each with its own arsenal of reasons, battle each other for supremacy of our minds. And our resulting decisions, whether bold or timid, well thought out or impulsive, can either set the course of action or blind it.

I don't have much advice to give you about decision-making, except this: Whatever you do, don't camp at the fork in the road. Decide. It's far better to make a wrong decision than to not make one at all. Each of us must confront our emotional turmoil and sort out our feelings.

As one young entrepreneur said to me after deciding to risk all and start a new business: "I have given up on the idea of getting rid of the butterflies in my stomach. But at least now I can make them fly in formation most of the time."

You, of course, have a tremendous tool for decision-making, right? If you did the exercises on goal-setting (You did, didn't you? If not, it's not too late to do them now), you have a long-range and short-range plan for your life. All you have to do now is decide to act by showing the proper *desire*.

Desire

How does one gain desire? I don't think I can answer this directly because there are many ways. But I do know two things about desire:

1. It comes from the inside not the outside.

2. It can be triggered by outside forces.

Almost anything can trigger desire. It's a matter of timing as much as preparation. It might be a song that tugs at the heart. It might be a memorable sermon. It might be a movie, a conversation with a friend, a confrontation with an enemy, or a bitter experience. Even a book such as this one can trigger the inner mechanism that will make some people say, "I want it now!"

Therefore, while searching for your "hot button" of pure, raw desire, welcome into your life each positive experience. Don't erect a wall to protect you from experiencing life. The same wall that keeps out disappointment also keeps out the sunlight of enriching experiences. So let life touch you. The next touch could be the one that turns your life around.

Resolve

Resolve says, "I will." These two words are among the most potent in the English language. I WILL.

Benjamin Disraeli, the great British statesman, once said, "Nothing can resist a human will that will stake even its existence on the extent of its purpose." In other words, when someone resolves to "do or die," nothing can stop him.

The mountain climber says, "I will climb the mountain. They've told me it's too high, it's too far, it's too steep, it's too rocky, it's too difficult. But it's *my* mountain. I *will* climb it. You'll soon see me waving from the top or you'll never see me, because unless I reach the peak, I'm not coming back." Who can argue with such resolve!

When confronted with such iron-willed determination, I can see Time, Fate, and Circumstance calling a hasty conference and deciding, "We might as well let him have his dream. He said he's going to get there or die trying."

The best definition for "resolve" I've ever heard came from a schoolgirl in Foster City, California. As is my custom, I was lecturing about success to a group of bright kids at a junior high school. I asked, "Who can tell me what 'resolve' means?" Several hands went up, and I did get some pretty good definitions. But the last was the best. A shy girl from the back of the room got up and said with quiet intensity, "I think resolve means promising yourself you will never give up." That's it! That's the best definition I've ever heard: PROMISE YOUR-SELF YOU'LL NEVER GIVE UP.

Think about it! How long should a baby try to learn how to walk? How long would you give the average baby before you say, "That's it, you've had your chance"? You say that's crazy? Of course it is. Any mother in the world would say, "My baby is going to keep trying *until* he learns how to walk!" No wonder everyone walks.

There is a vital lesson in this. Ask yourself, "How long am I going to work to make my dreams come true?" I suggest you answer, "As long as it takes." That's what resolve is all about.

★ ACTION ★

Knowledge fueled by emotion equals action. Action is the last part of the formula. It's the ingredient that ensures results. Only action can cause reaction. Further, only positive action can cause positive reaction.

Action. The whole world loves to watch those who make things happen, and it rewards them for causing waves of productive enterprise.

I stress this because today I see many people who are really sold on affirmations. And yet there is a famous saying that "Faith without action serves no useful purpose." How true!

I have nothing against affirmations as a tool to create action. Repeated to reinforce a disciplined plan, affirmations can help create wonderful results.

But there is also a very thin line between faith and folly. You see, affirmations without action are the beginnings of self-delusion. And for your well-being, there is little worse than self-delusion. It's like the sales executive who comes out of a sales meeting all revved up and says, "I'm going to be the biggest in the business," but then puts no disciplined thought or action behind her words. She might as well be walking west looking for the sunrise.

★ FOUR QUESTIONS ★

As we approach the end of our journey together, I have some questions I want you to ponder. The first is: Why should you try? Children often ask "why" questions. And this is an important "why" question. I mean, why get up early? Why work so hard? Why read that many books? Why make that many friends? Why go that far? Why earn that much? Why give that much away?

The best answer to the "Why should you try?" question is another question: *Why not*? What else are you going to do with your life? Why not see how far you can go? Why not see how much you can earn, or read, or share? Why not see what you can become or how much you can grow? Why not? After all, you'll be here until you go. Why not stay here in style?

The third question goes a bit further. It demands: "Why not you?" Some people have done the most incredible things with a limited background. Some people do so well that they get to see it all. Why not you?

Why not you watching the morning mist over the Hebrides Islands off Scotland? Why not you soaking up history in the Tower of London or exploring the dark mysteries of Spain? Why not you having lunch in one of those charming cafes overlooking the famous Champs Elysees in Paris? Why not you?

There is nothing like a stroll through the Hall of Mirrors at the palace of Versailles or gazing at the Mona Lisa in the Louvre.

Why not you sailing a schooner in the Caribbean? Do you know where the most exquisite seashells are in Miami? I can show you.

Why not you shopping on Fifth Avenue in New York City, staying at the Waldorf or the Plaza or the Carlisle, having sliced roast goose on a bed of apple strudel at Luchow's? Why not you drinking in the Arizona sunset? Why not you enjoying all that life has to offer, knowing that it is your reward for disciplined and consistent effort?

Why not you?

And now, my friend, here's my last question to you: Why not now? Why postpone a better future when so much that is wondrous awaits your command? Get at it today. Get some new books, make your detailed goal plan, take a millionaire out to lunch, find new ways to increase your productivity, develop a lifestyle of generosity and love, make a new effort to believe in yourself. And get moving.

Finally, ask for God's help. Yes, I believe our future success is up to us. But I also know that we all need spiritual sustenance, especially when our resolve weakens as we face adversity.

There is a story about a man who took a rock pile and in two years turned it into a lovely garden filled with the most beautiful flowers. One day a holy man came by. He had heard about the garden, as its fame spread for miles around. But he also wanted to make sure the gardener didn't forget the ultimate Creator. So he said, "Gardener, the Lord has certainly blessed you with a beautiful garden." The gardener understood. "You're right, holy man," he said. "If it weren't for the sunshine, the rain, the soil, and the miracle of the seed and the seasons, there would be no garden at all. But you should have seen this place a couple of years ago when God had it all to Himself."

You and I have been given the gifts of life, but it's up to us to decide if we are going to use God's laws to create and to prosper.

HOW TO USE A JOURNAL

You have just read about the importance of keeping a journal. Now listen to Jim Rohn as he explains **in detail** how to make your journal a "textbook for better living," positively affecting your quest for wealth and happiness.

This program includes two cassette tapes and a handsome journal for your personal use .... Only $30 U.S.
(see order form)

AN EVENING WITH JIM ROHN — Videocassette

With this video, you can experience Jim giving one of his famous talks. Covering some of his most popular topics, this 45-minute videocassette is a great intro into Jim's world of ideas and action. Ideal for self-study and for training meetings and seminars.

Available in VHS or Beta. **SAVE $26!** This program normally retails for $115. Special for this book .. Only $89 U.S.
(see order form)

SPECIAL OFFER

SAVE AN ADDITIONAL $28! ORDER THE COMPLETE SET OF ITEMS, INCLUDING THE **STRATEGIES** TAPE ALBUM, THE **JOURNAL** PROGRAM, AND THE **EVENING** VIDEO WITH A COMBINED RETAIL VALUE OF $210 AND RECEIVE A TOTAL OF $54 OFF REGULAR PRICE. .... ONLY $169 U.S.

ORDER FORM

Dear People at Prima: I'd like to order the following books/cassettes from you:

Quantity	Title	Unit Cost	Total
_____	7 Strategies . . . (Cassettes)	$ 65.00*	$_____
_____	How to Use a Journal	$ 30.00*	$_____
_____	An Evening with . . . (Video) ☐ VHS ☐ BETA (check one)	$ 89.00*	$_____
_____	**SAVE $$$!! ALL 3 FOR ONLY $169.95***		$_____
_____	7 Strategies . . . . (Book)	$ 13.95*	$_____
Subtotal			$_____
CA sales tax (if applicable)			$_____
Shipping: Allow 4 weeks. (Foreign orders: for AIR MAIL only, we'll charge exact postage to your Visa/MC plus $3 handl.)			$_____3.00
TOTAL TO BE REMITTED			$_____

* A great gift idea!

HOW TO ORDER: By telephone: With Visa/MC, call (916) 624-5718. Phone orders are taken Mon.-Fri., 9 a.m.-4 p.m. Pacific time.

By mail: Just fill out the information below and send with your remittance.

I am paying by (check one):   ☐ Check   ☐ MO   ☐ Visa/MC.

My name is _____

I live at _____

City _____ State _____ Zip _____

Visa/MC # _____ Expiration _____

Signature _____

PRIMA PUBLISHING
POST OFFICE BOX 1260R
ROCKLIN, CA 95677-1260
(Satisfaction unconditionally guaranteed.)